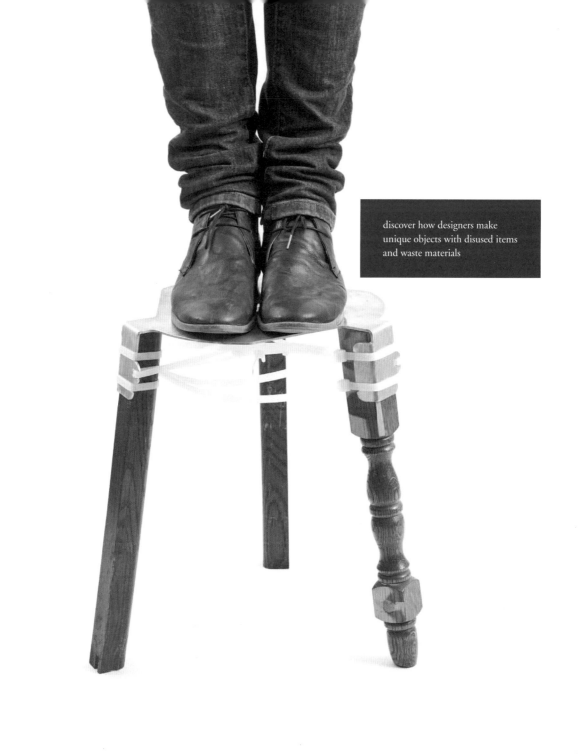

discover how designers make
unique objects with disused items
and waste materials

On the front cover:
Sign Stool by Trent Jansen Studio.
Photograph by Alex Kershaw.
See more on page 164.

On the back cover:
My Family by Sonia Verguet.
Photograph by Sonia Verguet.
See more on page 154.

ElasticShelf by SystemDesignStudio.
Photograph courtesy of SystemDesignStudio.
See more on page 104.

Weld Vases by Phil Cuttance.
Photographs by Pter Krecji unless otherwise stated.
See more on page 036.

On the spine:
Multi-vase Lighting by Atelier Remy & Veenhuizen.
Photograph courtesy of Atelier Remy & Veenhuizen.
See more on page 214.

On page 001:
Bender Stool by Paul Evermann.
Photograph by Matthias Ritzmann.
See more on page 096.

On pages 004 and 005:
Wildfor Lamp by Fordesignfor.
Photograph courtesy of Serena Riccardi.
See more on page 246.

On pages 008 and 009:
Beautiful Planets by Béatrix Li-Chin Loos for Galerie Gosserez.
Photograph by Maxime Champion.
See more on page 032.

On pages 094 and 095:
Bolt Furniture by Jamison Sellers.
Photograph by Jamison Sellers.
See more on page 150.

On pages 212 and 213:
Hanger Lamp by Luís Teixeira / 1961ecodesign. Photograph by
Fabrice Ziegler.
See more on page 228.

On page 288:
Relumine by mischer'traxler.
Photograph by mischer'traxler.
See more on page 216.

Upcycle!
© 2012 an\b editions (Singapore)

USA/Europe edition published by
Gingko Press Inc.
1321 Fifth Street
Berkerly, California 94710, USA
Phone: (510) 898-1195
Fax: (510) 898-1196
books@gingkopress.com
www.gingkopress.com

Produced by: an\b editions (Singapore)
Publishers: Abdul Nasser and Jacinta Sonja Neoh
Editorial Coordination and Text: Narelle Yabuka
Art Direction: Jacinta Sonja Neoh
Design and Layout: Lara SH Loi
Printed by: Tiger Printing (Hong Kong) Co., Ltd

ISBN: 978-1-58423-468-5

Up

cycle!

More than 100
upcycling ideas for
furniture,
lighting,
products, and
accessories!

GINGKO PRESS

contents

introduction

As opposed to recycling or downcycling, upcycling involves converting an object into something of greater value without degrading the material with which it is made. This alternate approach to the reuse of waste materials and disused objects requires a much smaller input of energy for the processing of the material, and leaves open the possibility of using the material again in the future.

The term 'upcycling' has been used since at least 1999, when it appeared as the title of a German-language book on the subject written by Gunter Pauli and Johannes F. Hartkemeyer. It has gained wider currency since, with its popularity fueled by marketing and discussion about 'green' lifestyles. Upcycling has fast become a popular at-home craft, promoting reuse at a domestic scale. As an approach to the design and manufacture of consumer objects, upcycling holds even greater potential for reduced reliance on new material resources. It also encourages an approach to form-making that challenges our preconceptions about design and the aesthetics of form.

The use of found objects and collage has a long history in twentieth-century art. Many exciting new ideas have been suggested through decontextualisation and the unexpected

combination of different elements. Contemporary designers such as Tejo Remy, Jurgen Bey, Estudio Campana, and Martino Gamper take a similar approach. They often arrive at furniture forms that shock and surprise, deliberately undermining stylistic conventions.

Tejo Remy – whose recent work (with René Veenhuizen) is featured in this book – designed the Rag Chair, You Can't Lay Down Your Memory (a chest of drawers), and Milkbottlelamp (all distributed by Droog) with reclaimed materials twenty years ago in 1991. The idea of radical reinvention and the recollection of memory drove this work, though today we might also view it through the lens of ecological sustainability. Tejo's current work continues to explore the creation of new meanings and aims to engage object users mentally and emotionally.

This book aims to illustrate the conceptual richness that can accompany a sustainable approach to design. It surveys the use of upcycling by professional designers (as well as some artists) in the areas of furniture, lighting, home products, and accessories. Investigation into this recent work reveals an array of factors that have influenced creative output – from concerns about landfill to the expression of local identity. More than 100 projects are featured, originating in a diverse group of countries including Brazil, Poland, Singapore, the Czech Republic, Israel, South Africa, Japan, the Netherlands, the UK, and Australia.

Whether you are a designer or a would-be upcycler, we hope that this book offers you an abundance of inspiration for creativity and experimentation that is sustainable in many ways.

(L–R) Rag Chair, You Can't Lay Down Your Memory, and Milkbottlelamp by Tejo Remy (distributed by Droog), 1991; the parts of old furniture prior to being sliced to create Oormerk's Replex veneer (see more on page 140). Photographs (L–R) by Hans van der Mars, Bob Goedewagen, Marcel Loermans, and Roel van de Laar.

01. products and accessories

animal skin rugs

by Agustina Woodgate

Photographs courtesy of Agustina Woodgate and Spinello Projects

How do stories, traditions, and rituals influence our relationships with what surrounds us? Artist Agustina Woodgate has investigated the connections between archetypal narratives and individual stories with a series of rugs made from disassembled stuffed animal toys. Fragments of the skins of pre-loved toys are stitched together into puzzles of fur that reference traditional rug designs.

\01: Agustina working in her studio on the rug titled *Royal*. The fur fragments are used without modifications to their shape.

The project began with Agustina's contemplation of her own childhood teddy bear Pepe, and a song written for him by her grandmother. She deconstructed four bears, unpicking the stitching and removing the stuffing until she was left with a collection of fur pieces. She organised the pieces into groups of the same kind (for example, paws), and designed a rug with its own formal pattern language.

Agustina Woodgate (Miami, USA) is an interdisciplinary artist. She studied fine arts in her hometown of Buenos Aires, Argentina, and has been based in Florida since 2005. She creates art that fosters exchanges between people rather than encounters between a viewer and object. Her intention is that through these exchanges, meaning is elaborated collectively rather than in the space of individual consumption. Portrait by Anthony Spinello.

www.agustinawoodgate.com

Animal Skin Rugs by Agustina Woodgate

\02: *No Rain No Rainbows* is the largest of the rugs, measuring 16 x 9.5ft (approximately 5 x 3m).

Keen to explore the possibilities further, Agustina embarked on a collection process through which she garnered used stuffed animals from friends, families, and various other communities. By virtue of their former status as treasured objects, each of the animals could be viewed as an archive of personal stories and memories. Simultaneously, they could be looked upon as subjects of sacrifice and abandon.

The Animal Skin Rugs place these personal histories alongside references to the broader social meanings found within traditional rug designs – particularly those of Eastern cultures, which often depict aspects of a people's spiritual and mental world. The collision of the personal and the collective encourages us to ponder our own memories and their meanings.

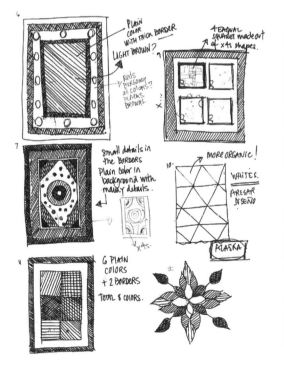

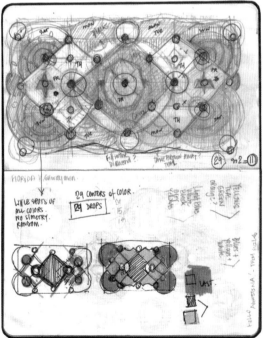

Animal Skin Rugs by Agustina Woodgate

the dreyfuss special

by Uncle Oswald Is My Hero

Photographs courtesy of Uncle Oswald Is My Hero

One of the most enduring creations of American industrial designer Henry Dreyfuss (1904–1972) was a series of telephones that were used all over the world for decades. They were made with Bakelite – an early type of non-biodegradable plastic. Although these telephones have now been superseded by technology and design, they continue to persist. Regrettably, today their longevity has a very different connotation.

\01: The speaker allows the younger generation to use a product that was once used by their parents and grandparents.

The Dreyfuss Special is a stereo speaker system for digital music players that uses the familiar Dreyfuss-designed handset. The size, structure, and shape of the handset's receiving and transmitting chambers were designed by Dreyfuss for optimum audio performance. Thus, the transition to a speaker function was straightforward, with no modifications required to the handset form. The speakers, the designers assure, sound brilliant.

Justin Kim (London, UK) and Jinsop Lee (Seoul, South Korea) met during their compulsory military service in South Korea. Preoccupying themselves with future plans, they agreed to establish a design company together. They also agreed that "Uncle Oswald" (the name of a hedonistic character in Roald Dahl stories) would form part of the company name, and that they would have a lot of fun! Portrait courtesy of Uncle Oswald Is My Hero.

www.uncleoswald.com

The Dreyfuss Special by Uncle Oswald Is My Hero

\02: The handset chamber faceplates are also reused, forming the casing for the plug components.

accidental carpet

by Atelier Remy & Veenhuizen
in collaboration with Tanja Smeets

Photographs courtesy of Atelier Remy & Veenhuizen

The Accidental Carpet puts old woollen blankets to task in the provision of warmth and comfort, but in a manner that differs greatly from their typical function. Each thirty-millimetre-thick Accidental Carpet is a composition of strips of blanket that are glued together and attached to a backing. Being handmade with blankets available at the time of production, each carpet is a unique configuration of colour and pattern.

\01: Like the folds of the brain, strips of old blanket curl and wrap in formations that are unique to each carpet.

The variable design refers to the structure of the brain, and was conceived as a playful, flowing mass. The first Accidental Carpet was created to bring a dose of cheer – as well as a soft, comfortable spot – to an institutional space used by children with epilepsy.

Tejo Remy and René Veenhuizen (Utrecht, The Netherlands) work together as product, interior, and public space designers. Their key preoccupation is to explore the possibilities inherent in found goods and materials – and to create new meanings by using them in alternate ways and contexts. Tanja Smeets (Utrecht, The Netherlands) is an artist who creates 'hyperorganic' sculptures with uncommon industrial materials as well as materials from everyday life. Accidental Carpet was the trio's first collaboration. Portraits courtesy of Atelier Remy & Veenhuizen and Tanja Smeets.

www.remyveenhuizen.nl
www.tanjasmeets.nl

Accidental Carpet by Atelier Remy & Veenhuizen in collaboration with Tanja Smeets

\02: The transformed blankets create a comforting spot to rest – a soft form made with a soft material.

abitudini

by Antonello Fusè for Resign

Photographs by Alice Brandolini

With Abitudini, an old habit dies hard while broken chairs live on. "Abitudini" means "habits" or "customs" in Italian. "Abiti" means "clothes." Abitudini hangers play on the habit of hanging one's coat or jacket on the back of their chair. The tops of chair backs are cut to various lengths and restored before custom-designed hooks are attached. The result is a sturdy hanger ideal for heavy, bulky clothing.

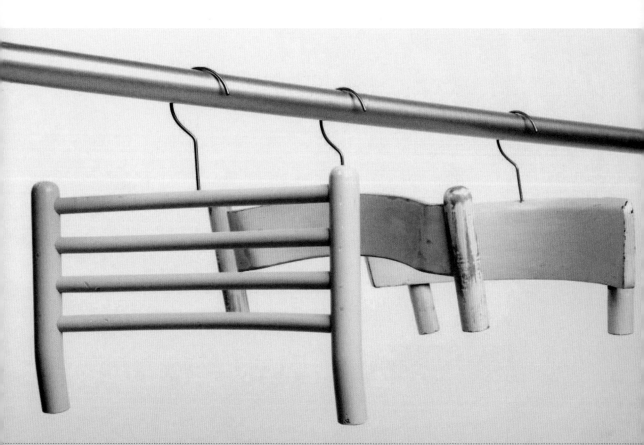

\01: Although the chair backs are restored, signs of past use (such as chips in paintwork) are allowed to persist.

Resign (Faenza, Italy) is a "meta-project" consisting of a physical atelier space and a network of relationships. At its core is the promotion of a sustainable approach to design – from both an environmental and social perspective. Objects are regarded not from an aesthetic point of view, but with consideration of their ability to create human relationships and express identity. The Resign project facilitates design activities, research, education and training, and professional advice.

Industrial designer Antonello Fusè (Vanzago, Italy) worked in the field of car design before finding resonance with Resign's "design alchemy," as he describes it. Antonello graduated from the Nuova Accademia Di Belle Arti Milano in 2008. During his studies, his work was shown in exhibitions of design and street art. Portrait courtesy of Resign.

www.resign.it

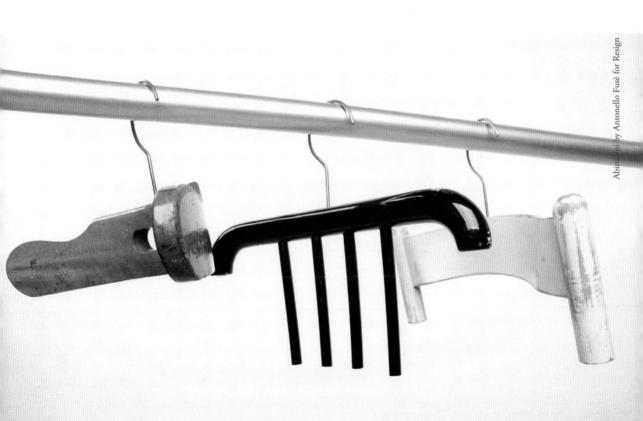

Abitudini by Antonello Fusè for Resign

\02: Shapes familiar in the context of furniture become surprising in the context of the clothes hanger.

\03: Abitudini hangers play with the widely recognised symbolic value of chair backs as places to hang one's clothes.

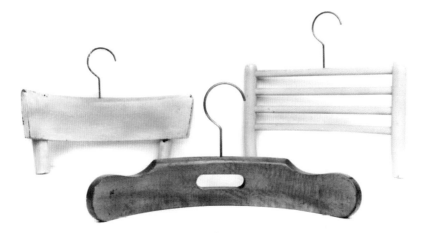

Abitudini by Antonello Fusè for Resign

Resign promotes new meanings
through a "re-use of signs" – a
creative recombination of the
signs (or meanings) embedded
in discarded objects.

\04: The varied design characteristics of the chairs subtly persist thanks to a tailored cutting approach.

bi-re-cycle jewellery

by Nikolay Sardamov

Photographs by Aleksandar Nishkov

Bi-re-cycle Jewellery grants the discarded rubber inner tubes of bicycles a new purpose and value. Formerly hidden from view within bicycle tyres, the inner tubes are revealed and celebrated in this abstract unisex jewellery. The tough, malleable quality of the rubber is expressed in various ways; it is sliced, punctured, and stretched over skeletal silver frameworks to create abstract works of wearable art.

\01: The inherent structural quality of the tubing is both challenged (in earrings and brooches) and utilised (in a layered necklace).

The necklaces, brooches, and earrings in the range were inspired by mobility, and play on a shape of eternal importance in jewellery – the circle. Reuse is an equally significant component of the work. Recycling and reuse, says designer Nikolay Sardamov, will play a significant role in the future intelligent society as well as in jewellery design.

Nikolay Sardamov (Sofia, Bulgaria) studied fine arts pedagogy before achieving a master's degree in jewellery and metal. He has held solo exhibitions since 2001. The circle is a repeating theme in Nikolay's jewellery, and silver is a favoured material – often in blackened form, which lends an industrial feel to the work. Portrait by Vencislava Vasileva and Asen Emilov.

www.sardamov.com

Bi-re-cycle Jewellery by Nikolay Sardamov

\03: Brooches (above) and earrings (to the right) reveal the strength and transformative quality of rubber.

Nikolay began working with bicycle inner tubes after discovering a bicycle repair shop's used tyre stockpile. He considered the tubes as a raw material for jewellery production and began experimenting. In doing so, he discovered a material that offered limitless inspiration.

The pairing of discarded rubber inner tubes with precious silver throws into question established notions about the value of materials in the context of jewellery.

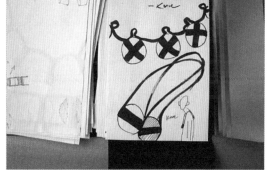

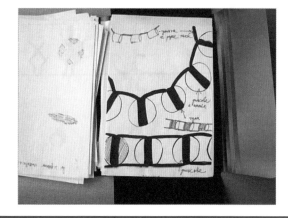

Bi-re-cycle Jewellery by Nikolay Sardamov

menorah

by Reddish Studio

Photographs by Dan Lev and Reddish Studio

A menorah is a traditional Jewish candelabrum. In its seven-branched form, it is used in the Temple in Jerusalem and is a symbol of Judaism and the state of Israel. In its nine-branched form, it is used on the Jewish holiday of Hanukkah. It has been a symbol of unity since ancient times. Offering a new expression of togetherness, Israeli design studio Reddish has designed a contemporary menorah using old candlesticks.

\01: The simple white metal frame encloses diverse and complex forms, and raises every candlestick to the same level.

The designers collected a variety of single candlesticks from Israeli flea markets. The pairs from which the reclaimed candlesticks were lost would once have played an important role in family ceremonies. The diversity of metals and styles (from different eras) is regarded by the designers as an appropriate reflection of Israeli society. The contrasting candlesticks are framed by and suspended from a unifying iron frame.

Designers Naama Steinbock and Idan Friedman founded Reddish Studio (Sitriya, Israel) in 2002. The studio produces a variety of objects including furniture, lighting, home accessories, and jewellery. No matter the type of object, Naama and Idan strive to infuse each one with its own character – something with which people can find a personal connection. Photograph by Shay Ben-Efraim.

www.reddishstudio.com

Menorah by Reddish Studio

\02: The individual candlesticks, which would have originated in different parts of the world, represent a community within the white frame.

bow bins

by Cordula Kehrer

Photographs by Cordula Kehrer and Evi Künstle

The obsession with newness that has marked our era is thoroughly challenged by Cordula Kehrer's Bow Bins. Her project of renewal involves the mending and reinvention of damaged plastic buckets, bowls, and tubs with weaving. Willow, rush, and rattan are hand-woven onto the plastic fragments by local German basket makers. Every bin is unique.

\01: Fragments of damaged plastic vessels are repaired and grafted with weaving.

Bow Bins involve a fusion of mass-produced synthetic plastic vessels with replications of counterparts that have enjoyed a far longer history. It is a startling reminder of our changed material culture and methods of production. Cordula's engagement of Germany-based weavers is also poignant, serving as a reminder of the widespread disappearance of such crafts from industrialised societies.

Cordula Kehrer (Karlsruhe, Germany) studied design in Germany (at the University of Media, Art and Design in Karlsruhe) and in Japan (at the Kyushu Institute of Design). She has been working independently for several years. Cordula likes to explore new ways of living in the constantly changing world, and works with a perception of sustainability that relates to both material and culture. Portrait courtesy of Cordula Kehrer.

www.cordulakehrer.de

Bow Bins by Cordula Kehrer

\02: A variety of weaving styles are used, enhancing the uniqueness of each bin.

Bow Bins suggest a way to make better use of our existing material resources. They also offer a way to keep traditional crafts alive with the assurance of fair and reasonable returns for labour.

Bow Bins are handmade in Germany by local basket makers Carolin Ebert, Anja van Kempen, Claudia Rieger, Ilse Walther, and Lore Wild.

\03: The woven material is anchored to the plastic in various ways and junctions take on a number of characteristics.

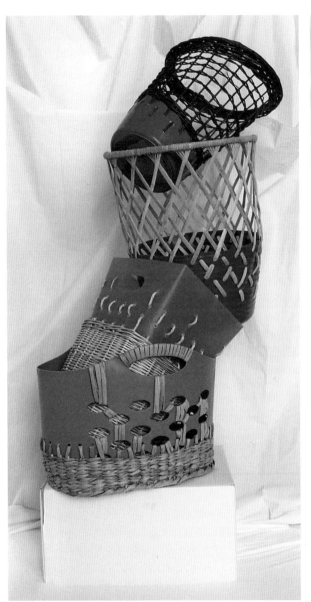

Bow Bins by Cordula Kehrer

\04: The proliferation of discarded plastic items leads to the potential for series of Bow Bins.

beautiful planets

by Béatrix Li-Chin Loos for Galerie Gosserez

Photographs by Maxime Champion

An ecological imperative informed both the shape and material of the Beautiful Planets – a series of sculptural vases made with offcuts of elm and chipboard, reclaimed cardboard boxes, and reclaimed leather. Each vase represents a different planet. The subtext – reinforced by the engraved motto "mother earth" (or "la terre est notre mère" in French) – is a message about our duty of care for our planet.

\01: A lacquered central layer represents planetary rings. The reclaimed leather strap is marked with the word "reuse."

The fragments of reclaimed wood and cardboard are layered like rock strata. Their choreography generates intricate contrasting patterns of wood grains and corrugations. At the centre of each vase, a blown glass tube holds water and mimics a planetary axis. The axial tilt hints at the orbital systems of which all planets are a part. The vases range in diameter from 150 to 280 millimetres and were created exclusively for Galerie Gosserez in Paris.

Béatrix Li-Chin Loos (Strasbourg, France) has spent some years torn between ecological campaigning and creative pursuits. She studied architecture, social sciences, and environmental policy before joining Greenpeace and voyaging on the Rainbow Warrior. Thereafter, she worked for various environmental charities before undertaking a cabinet-making course at the École Boulle in Paris. She created her first collection of objects made with scrap materials in 2009. Portrait courtesy of Galerie Gosserez.

www.chutcollections.fr
www.galeriegosserez.com

Beautiful Planets by
Béatrix Li-Chin Loos for Galerie Gosserez

\02: Raw and finished surfaces are deliberately contrasted. Chipboard, sanded and painted silver, begins to resemble volcanic rock.

bullet rings

by Adi Zaffran Weisler

Photographs by Adi Zaffran Weisler

The smooth, streamlined, and perfected form of an unused bullet is charged with an alarming potential. An expression of that strong capacity lingers in the contorted forms of spent bullets. Their journey and transformation is recorded in powerfully forged shards and bulbs of metal. The tragic beauty of these forms, and the degree of force that produced them, is thrust into focus by the confronting Bullet Rings.

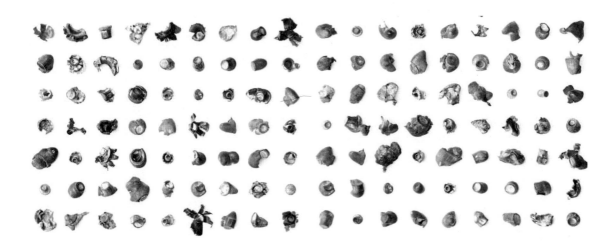

\01: The contorted forms of the spent bullets – infinite in their variety – convey the history of each round fired.

The jewellery was made with spent bullets collected from a firing range in Rehovot, Israel. Attached to simple bands of unpolished copper in a traditional composition, the spent bullets are bestowed with a precious jewel-like status. The altered context emphasises the unconventional beauty inherent in the deformed shapes. It also encourages an unavoidable contemplation of their history.

Product designer Adi Zaffran Weisler (Tel Aviv-Yafo, Israel) recently graduated from the industrial design department of Bezalel Academy of Arts and Design in Jerusalem, where he is now a teaching assistant. Adi undertakes design work both independently and with Four&Five designgroup – a Tel Aviv-Yafo-based product design studio composed of Bezalel alumni. He is also an instructor in a preparatory school for design students. Portrait courtesy of Adi Zaffran Weisler.

www.adizaffran.com

Bullet Rings by Adi Zaffran Weisler

\02: The jagged, unpolished nature of the rings is as confronting as the material with which they are made.

weld vases

by Phil Cuttance

Photographs by Pter Krecji unless otherwise stated

Plastic objects are typically mass-manufactured by machines, with the material being moulded into any number of shapes. Manipulating it in sheet form and forging one's own joints – as though welding sheet metal – is a significant departure from typical practice. For designer Phil Cuttance, it was an imperative given his dedication to the use of waste rather than virgin plastic.

\01: The handmade quality of the welded joints brings rare idiosyncrasies to objects made of plastic.

The Weld Vases are produced by welding offcuts of ABS plastic that were discarded by a London plastic fabricator. Phil discovered hot air plastic welding during a visit to a car bumper repair shop, and was immediately inspired to experiment.

New Zealand-born designer Phil Cuttance (now based in London, UK) has been designing and making furniture and objects for over ten years. He had hankered to create objects using the technique of hot air plastic welding, but was uncomfortable about using new material. His discovery of the discarded offcuts created the opportunity to experiment with the process. Portrait courtesy of Phil Cuttance.

www.philcuttance.com

Weld Vases by Phil Cuttance

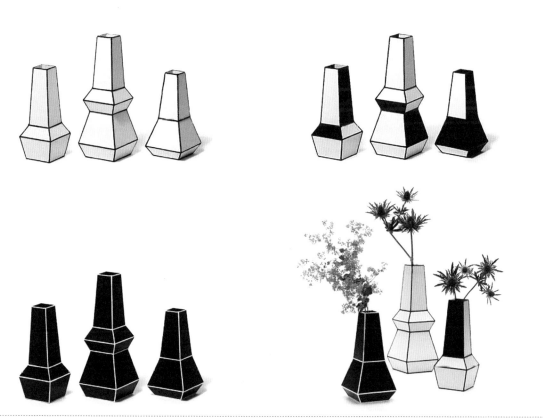

Hot air welding creates strong and decorative edges while joining the thin plastic shapes together. The technique involves the use of a hot air welding gun, which produces a jet of hot air to soften the two parts as well as a plastic filler rod. The technique is often used to weld together the parts of a broken plastic object (such as a car bumper).

The vases are produced in three shapes and three tonal combinations. They are welded using a contrasting colour, which draws attention to the handmade process. Being individually handcrafted, the Weld Vases are idiosyncratic and therefore possess an inherent value that is unusual for plastic goods. Playing on this notion of value, each vase is individually numbered on its base.

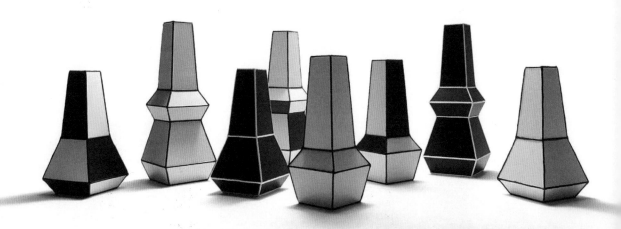

\03: Three shapes are produced: tall (37 x 13.5cm), high-waist (26 x 13cm), and low-waist (28 x 12cm).

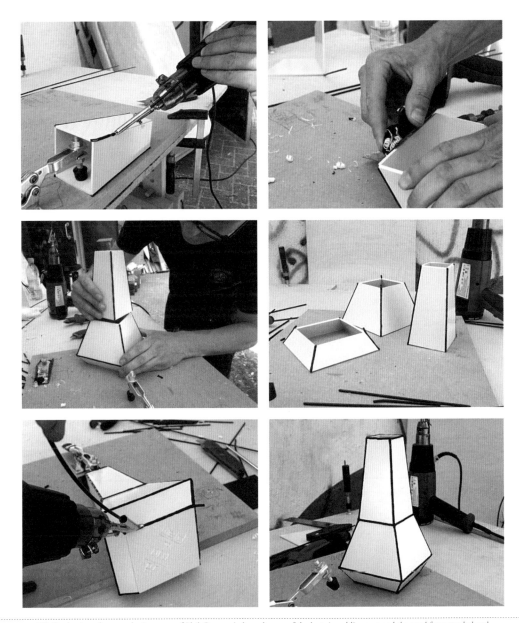

Weld Vases by Phil Cuttance

\04: Production photographs (courtesy of Phil Cuttance) show the use of the hot air welding gun and the need for a steady hand.

recycle shoes

by Liza Fredrika Åslund
for What's More Alive Than You
Photographs courtesy of What's More Alive Than You

Abstract collages of furniture fragments ironically provide stable footing for wearers of What's More Alive Than You's Recycle Shoes. The unconventional heels of these tanned goatskin shoes are made by hand, and each one is unique. The wooden fragments – upcycled from disused chairs and tables – are mounted on an iron pin, painted, and securely fastened to the heel of the shoe to create a single body.

\01: The shoes are available in three models, each of which caters to a different season. All contain vivid orange lining.

The shoes were designed in response to a bi-annual creative call from What's More Alive Than You – a new Italian fashion brand that produces high-end shoes, bags, and contemporary jewellery. This unique company involves students and professionals of art, architecture, and interior and fashion design from over ninety countries in the design of its collections. Its goal is to produce long-lasting works of wearable art.

Swedish fashion designer Liza Fredrika Åslund (Nyköping, Sweden) is fascinated by imperfections in fashion rather than immaculate absolutes. Her exploration of irregularity struck a chord with What's More Alive Than You (Padova, Italy) – a unique fashion company that offers wearable objects more aligned with the world of art than the rules of traditional fashion. Mario Innocente is the CEO. "What's More Alive Than You" is a registered trademark. Portraits courtesy of What's More Alive Than You.

www.wmaty.com

Recycle Shoes by Liza Fredrika Åslund for What's More Alive Than You

Singer and jazz musician Esperanza Spalding wore a pair of pink Recycle Shoes at the Grammy Awards ceremony in 2011. What's More Alive Than You and Liza Fredrika Åslund (a recent graduate of The Danish Design School) could not have wished for better exposure of the design.

found object jewellery

by Melissa Cameron

Photographs by Melissa Cameron

An ever-changing palette of found objects feeds the practice of jewellery designer and maker Melissa Cameron. Her work is driven by a fascination with geometry and patterns – from the regular, rhythmic patterns that can be found in architecture to the seemingly random fractals of nature. Her found object jewellery, unlike her works made in regular sheet metal, combines patterns of her own design with those existing on many of the objects.

\01: *Marian's Compact: Radial Pattern* (2009) was formerly a brass powder compact. (Collection of Toowoomba Regional Gallery.)

Melissa methodically conceives and investigates pattern motifs using the computer-aided drawing program AutoCAD. Her drawings become the plans for her work – templates for a delicate process of drilling and then sawing by hand. Layer by layer, the sawn shapes are strung into three dimensions on fine stainless steel cable or silk thread. The resulting brooches and pendants use 'ornamental' or 'precious' objects in a new precious and ornamental context.

Melissa Cameron (Melbourne, Australia) was an interior designer before she shifted her focus to constructions of a much smaller size. She recently completed a master's degree in fine arts at Monash University and now practices independently as a jewellery designer and maker. As is architecture, her layered wearable constructions are forms as well as spaces. Portrait by Marc Morel.

www.melissacameron.net

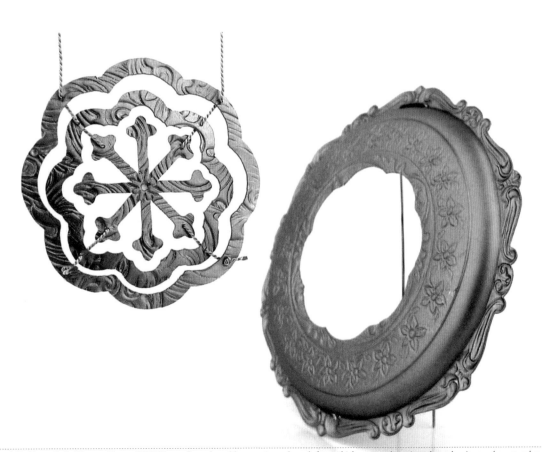

Found Object Jewellery by Melissa Cameron

\02: *Planar Radial Pattern, Coaster II* (2010) transformed an old coaster into a brooch from which two pendants (one shown here) were also cut and made.

\03: New forms were cut from an antique powder case and an old coaster to create *Eight Point Powder Case* and *Prato Coaster II* (both 2009).

The objects are obtained from markets, second-hand stores, and friends. Melissa enjoys the sense of engagement that jewellery made with found objects encourages in its wearer. The existing patterns allow the objects to be read as simultaneously old and new.

Found Object Jewellery by Melissa Cameron

\04: Intricate forms were created from cigarette and tobacco tins and a bamboo plate: *Red Tin Set*, *Bamboo Plate Set*, and *Tobacco Tin Set* (all 2009).

symbiosis

by Stanley Ruiz

Photographs courtesy of Stanley Ruiz

Improvisation drove the creation of Symbiosis – a pair of stereo speakers crafted with the scraps of wood that were lying around the designer's studio. Product designer Stanley Ruiz is fascinated with found objects – and with natural artifacts in particular – and he is constantly looking for ways to give these materials a second life.

\01: The speakers can be connected directly to portable digital music players – a confluence of craft and technology.

In Symbiosis, slats of scrap wood and a log were used in a direct, unprocessed manner to house the speaker components. The lo-fi design approach resulted in forms that speak of folk inspirations and intuition. The speed of construction is expressed in the irregular composition of slats (with deliberate misalignments), the unfinished condition of the log, and the use of zip ties and chunky wing nuts for the supporting structure.

Stanley Ruiz (New York, USA) has an extensive background in craft design and production. In his work, he fuses the industrial with the natural to encourage new interpretations and meanings for familiar objects. Stanley was born in the Filipino city of Manila. He lived in Bali (Indonesia) for several years, where he collaborated with village artisans and incorporated traditional handicrafts into his work. Portrait by CJ Rivera.

www.stanleyruiz.com

Symbiosis by Stanley Ruiz

\02: Steel rods, square-section steel tubes, and timber dowel and slats were choreographed into supporting frameworks.

\03: The speaker hardware was borrowed from the Ceramic Speakers designed by Joey Roth.

Stanley Ruiz believes that product design needn't be complicated. Nor should it be dependent upon the dictates of big marketing companies and manufacturers, he says.

Symbiosis by Stanley Ruiz

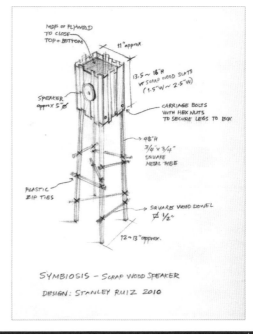

MDF or PLYWOOD TO CLOSE TOP + BOTTOM

11" approx

13.5 ~ 16"H w SCRAP WOOD SLATS (1.5"W ~ 2.5"W)

SPEAKER approx 5" ∅

CARRIAGE BOLTS WITH HEX NUTS TO SECURE LEGS TO BOX

48"H 3/4"x 3/4" SQUARE METAL TUBE

PLASTIC ZIP TIES

SQUARE WOOD DOWEL ∅ 1/2"

12~13"approx.

SYMBIOSIS - SCRAP WOOD SPEAKER

DESIGN: STANLEY RUIZ 2010

\04: There is an intentional visual discordance in the meeting of refined electrical components and a raw log.

cycle sign

by Trent Jansen Studio
Photographs copyright Alex Kershaw

Trent Jansen Studio's production of the Sign Stool 450 – a riveted seat made from reused road signs – results in a small amount of leftover material. Keen to use rather than waste the offcuts, the studio developed Cycle Sign – a reflector disc for bicycles that makes use of the colourful reflective scraps of signage in a direct and logical manner.

\01: Any existing scratches or scuffs on the reflective vinyl of the road signs are retained and celebrated.

Cycle Sign is produced in two formats. The double-sided clamp version can be easily attached to the spokes of a bicycle wheel. The single-sided strap version has been designed to wrap around the seat post or front tube of a bicycle frame. The philosophy of reuse was extended to the strap itself, which is cut from the rubber inner tubes of old bicycle tyres. The only new material used in the manufacture of Cycle Sign is felt padding.

After completing his studies at the College of Fine Arts, University of New South Wales in 2004, Trent Jansen (Sydney, Australia) interned at Marcel Wanders' Amsterdam studio. Trent established his own studio after returning to Australia later that year. His key aim is to practice "honest and poetic sustainable design" by developing objects of longevity that will maintain a lasting relationship with their users. Trent has also held teaching posts at several Australian universities. Portrait copyright Tobias Titz.

www.trentjansen.com

Cycle Sign by Trent Jansen Studio

Turn to page 164 to read about Trent Jansen Studio's Sign Stool 450.

\02: The strap version is fitted to the bicycle by wrapping the rubber strap around the seat post or frame and hooking it back on the disc.

pencil basket

by Stephen Bretland
Photographs by J. Sandiford

The Pencil Basket offers an unexpected new use for old, forgotten pencils. This playful, interactive fruit bowl is made with solid beech or birch plywood. A ring of slots at its perimeter allows pencils to be arranged in a lattice formation that prevents fruit from rolling off the base. Food-grade plant oil seals the timber to resist marking.

\01: The design encourages personalisation in terms of colour, height, and style.

The bowl was initially designed for *TEN XYZ* – an exhibition shown by the UK design collective TEN. The exhibition investigated whether digital technology is a sustainable option for the designer. The base of the Pencil Basket is manufactured using a three-axis CNC (computer numerical control) router, which can quickly machine profiles from digital files and eliminate tooling. This method minimises the raw materials used as well as the time and energy taken for production.

Stephen Bretland (Llandrillo, UK) is both an independent designer and a partner in the design company Loglike (which produces the Pencil Basket). Loglike designs and produces giftware, homewares, and t-shirts on a cottage-industry scale using natural and upcycled materials. Stephen's background is in furniture and product design, and he always addresses ethical and sustainability issues in his work. Portrait by J. Sandiford.

www.stephenbretland.com
www.loglike.co.uk

Pencil Basket by Stephen Bretland

\02: The size of the base is approximately 260 x 260 x 36mm. The timber is obtained from sustainable sources.

'second hand' plate series

by Karen Ryan

Photographs courtesy of Karen Ryan

A confrontational quality emanates from Karen Ryan's *'Second Hand' Plate* series. Single provocative words emerge from the congenial decorative scenes and patterns on old plates and platters. They prick our conscience and unsettle our state of mind. Karen's aim was to prise open hidden domestic realms, create portraits of them, and leave them bare for others to interpret.

\01: A rose emerges menacingly from the letter A on *'Second Hand' Hate Plate* (2006).

The plates are collected from a variety of contexts – jumble sales, car boot sales, charity shops, second-hand shops, and junk shops. Karen views the scenes and patterns as a form of camouflage in our everyday lives, and intentionally damages them. She sandblasts the plates to remove portions of the decorative surfaces. With the words and fragments she leaves behind, she aims to expose the darker and more secretive side of domestic life.

Karen Ryan (Portsmouth, UK) studied product and graphic design as well as fine art. A number of themes influence her creative practice – among them necessity, fate, autobiography, and subversion. She makes use of found materials that have assumed the status of 'waste' and makes one-off objects. The female story is also pivotal in Karen's designs, which collage old and new histories. Portrait by Fiona Wright.

www.bykarenryan.co.uk

'Second Hand' Plate Series by Karen Ryan

\02: A pair of birds assumes a new meaning in *'Second Hand' Lies Plate* (2009) – part of *Trilogy in Willow*.

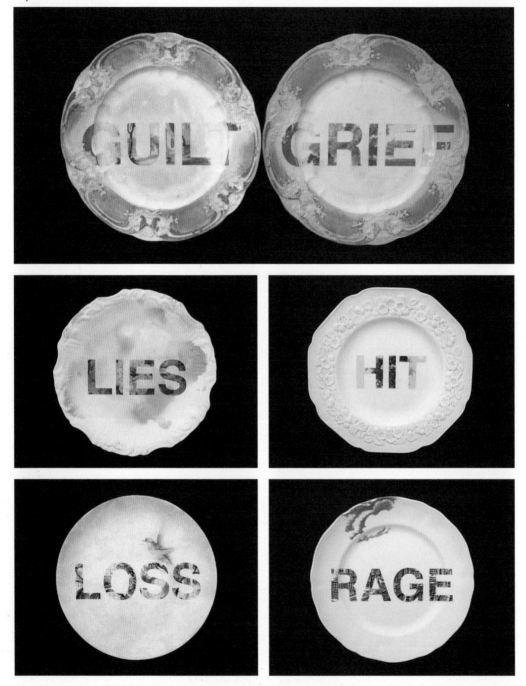

\03: 'Second Hand' Guilt and Grief Plates, Lies Plate, Hit Plate, Loss Plate, and Rage Plate (all 2007).

'Second Hand' Plate Series by Karen Ryan

\04: *'Second Hand' Beauty Plate* and *Forever Beloved Plate* (both 2009) – part of *Trilogy in Willow. 'Second Hand' Vanity Plate* and *Fear Plate* (both 2007).

mirador rings

by Bandada

Photographs by Bandada

"Mirador" is a Spanish word that refers to a place or space (natural or architectural) that is privileged for the contemplation of a landscape. Elevated lookout points are an example. Mirador Rings were inspired by the designers' observations of the geometry that composes new buildings in Barcelona. The circle and square create a strong asymmetrical form, with the protruding square hinting at the idea of a vantage point.

\01: The plywood rings resulted from experimentation with ways to combine industrial and craft processes with eco-friendly materials.

The design emphasises the side profile of layers of plywood offcuts. The scrap plywood – collected from a Barcelona carpenter and cut with a CNC machine – is teamed with colourful squares of melamine board reclaimed from an old sample book. Squares of gold, silver, and copper leaf were also used as a fun statement about the preciousness of jewellery. The plywood is sealed with varnish. A new series of rings and brooches – inspired by tangram puzzles – is currently being developed.

Bandada (Barcelona, Spain) is a jewellery brand established by Colombian-born designers Ana María Ramírez and Adriana Díaz Higuera. Ana María (left) studied fine arts, goldsmithing, jewellery design, and graphic design. Adriana (right) studied industrial design, silversmithing, jewellery design, and product design. Their varied creative backgrounds merge in their current practice, which seeks a balance between expression and functionality. Portraits by Bandada.

www.cuadernobandada.blogspot.com

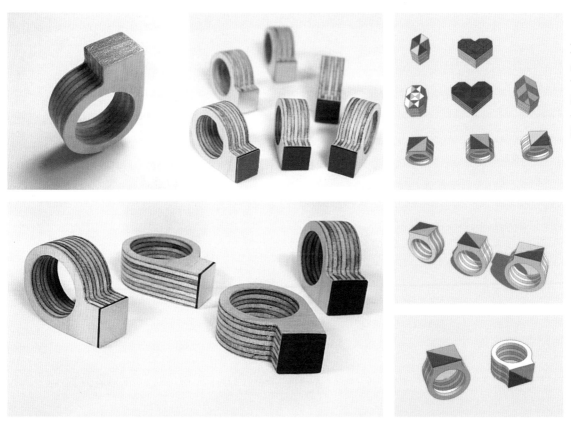

Mirador Rings by Bandada

coffee cuff

by Contexture Design

Product photographs by Contexture Design
Model photographs by Nik West

Small scraps of timber veneer from Vancouver's furniture industry are renewed and redefined to create the Coffee Cuff. When placed on the wrist, this dual-use product functions as a fashion accessory. When slipped onto a hot take-away coffee cup, it functions as a heat guard. Wood's natural insulating quality makes it an ideal material for the latter purpose, while the decorative effect of its grains also lend it to a fashion role.

\01: The reusable cuff can adapt to any typically sized coffee cup. Similarly, it can be worn around the wrist or forearm.

Contexture Design uses recycling principles in every step of the manufacturing process, which relies entirely on hand crafting. Discarded coffee cups are used as forms, and strips of punctured bicycle inner tubes (wrapped around the layers of veneer) provide even pressure during the laminating process. The veneer scraps available at the time of production determine the wood species used.

Designers Nathan Lee and Trevor Coghill work together as Contexture Design (Vancouver, Canada). The duo's approach to design emphasises simplicity and sustainability. Their work is often inspired by reclaimed materials that have historical, cultural, or environmental significance. Other products designed by Contexture include hanging mobiles made with salvaged road maps and iPod nano cases made from cassette tape shells. Portrait by Nik West.

www.contexture.ca

Coffee Cuff by Contexture Design

\02: One or two types of veneer compose each cuff. Timber species used to date include ebony, benge, and birdseye maple.

design help

by Lenka Křemenová, David Maštálka,
Marta Maštálková, and Petra Kasová

Product photographs courtesy of Design Help team
Model photograph by Jana Šprinclová

Many people assert that the atmosphere of healthcare environments is as important as the services provided within them. According to a group of young Czech architects and designers, the 'cold' atmosphere within the Haematology Department at Prague's Královské Vinohrady University Hospital required some serious improvement. They formed an association – Design Help – to do just that.

\01: Complimentary support was lent to the Design Help team by a photographer, stylist, and model.

In order to raise the money required for improvements, the group designed a jewellery collection with reclaimed and sanitised safe medical waste. Lengths of tubing, infusion lids, and other items were adapted and augmented to create original earrings, bracelets, and necklaces. Proceeds from the charitable sale of the jewellery are being used for Design Help improvement projects.

Design Help (Prague, Czech Republic) was founded by Lenka Křemenová (an architect), Marta Maštálková (a graphic designer), David Maštálka (an architect), and Petra Kasová (the team's manager). Design Help works in cooperation with the endowment fund Janele, which was established by a team of doctors and nurses from the hospital's Haematology Department. Portrait by Pavel Horák.

www.designhelp.cz

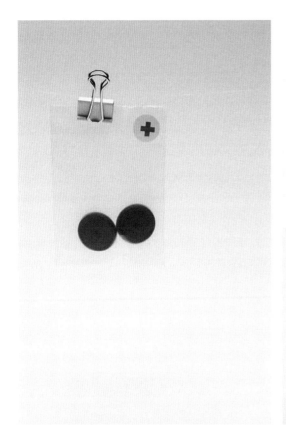

Design Help by Lenka Křemenová, David Maštálka, Marta Maštálková, and Petra Kasová

\02: Treated like precious stones, found objects – such as the red "flip-off" rubber lids from infusion bottles – were turned into earrings.

As part of the Design Help team, A1architects have designed a new interior for the main hall of the Inpatient Department at the hospital's Haematology Pavilion. The construction of the interior will be financially supported by the Design Help proceeds.

The Design Help project encourages contemplation of the vast amount of waste produced by the health-care industry, and the need for it to be properly managed.

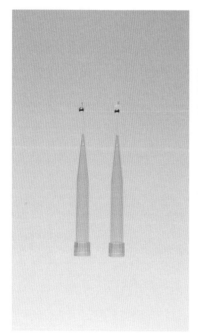

\03: Hanging earrings encourage the contemplation of health-care objects as valuable, sculptural items.

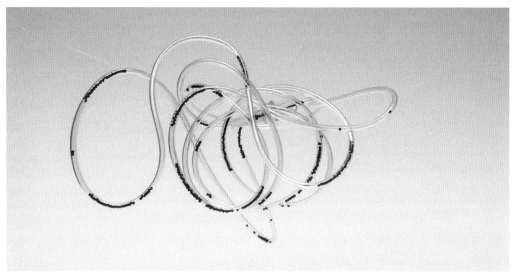

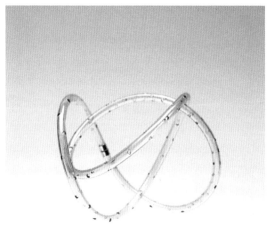

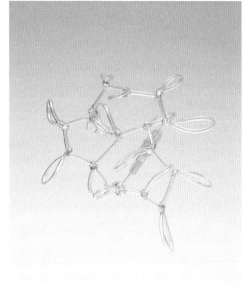

Design Help by Lenka Křemenová, David Maštálka, Marta Maštalíková, and Petra Kasová

\04: Tubing was punctured, tied, and manipulated into abstract necklaces and bracelets. Red beads add a confrontational quality.

message in a box

by Wendy Plomp

Photographs courtesy of Wendy Plomp

When studying how people create personal territory in public spaces, Wendy Plomp noticed how cardboard is often given spontaneous new functions – as a container for possessions; as a surface on which to sleep, beg, draw, or break-dance; or as a hitch-hiking sign. She had the idea of transforming cardboard boxes into disposable carpets that could instantly provide a clean space – even a sense a home – in any location.

\01: This detailed view of a carpet shows the intricacy of the silkcreened patterns.

Using water-based ink, she silkscreened ornate arabesque patterns onto the inside surfaces of recycled boxes. Humble pieces of cardboard took on the air of precious rugs. The form and size of each carpet was determined simply by the way each box was folded. Wendy perceives beauty in the graphic shapes of the unfolded boxes and hopes they encourage others to appreciate the unexpected.

Designer Wendy Plomp (Eindhoven, The Netherlands) is drawn to objects that have stories attached to them. Just as the exterior of a cardboard box reveals information about its contents, origin, and destination, Wendy sees great potential in the communicative properties of the interior – for example, as a means of transmitting information to the recipients of food drops in disaster areas. Portrait by Boudewijn Bollmann.

www.wnd.nu

Message in a Box by Wendy Plomp

\02: A cardboard box unfolds into a printed carpet. Each carpet is stamped with its number in the batch.

\03: Wendy has created special collections of carpets for the Italian gallery Spazio Rossana Orlandi and for private clients.

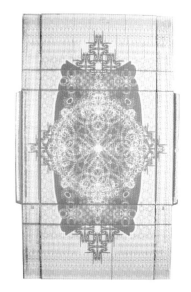

Message in a Box by Wendy Plomp

\04: The various formats are the result of simply unfolding differently shaped boxes.

chrysalis

by Lightly

Photographs by Cursor Ctrl unless otherwise stated

In the life cycle of the butterfly, the chrysalis is the transformative state undergone by the caterpillar before it reaches its mature form. Chrysalises will typically be attached to a vertical surface such as a leaf or twig, and when the butterfly emerges it will rest on the empty cocoon while it expands and hardens its wings. This natural cycle of renewal inspired the design of an ornamental product that brings new life to a discarded domestic item.

\01: The special collectors' range of Chrysalis is made from upcycled English collector saucers including Royal Doulton and Royal Vale designs.

The wall-mounted Chrysalis butterflies are made with upcycled ceramic and fine bone china saucers. Along with the imperative to work with discarded materials, two factors encouraged the use of saucers – their curved profile (which would cast shadows and suggest the movement of wings), and the delicacy of the material (which reflects the delicacy of a butterfly's wings). Designer Cindy-Lee Davies collects every saucer she uses and does not break up tea sets.

Cindy-Lee Davies (Melbourne, Australia) launched Lightly in 2005 in homage to her late grandmother. Her first products were homewares and lighting inspired by lace and doilies. The company now offers over eighty items that marry the aesthetics of traditional crafts with cutting-edge technology. Cindy-Lee's commitment to sustainable practice sees the bulk of Lightly products being made in Australia. Portrait by Cursor Ctrl.

www.lightly.com.au

Since 2009, Lightly has upcycled 8,000–10,000 saucers from discarded crockery stock in Australia, and over 5,000 saucers that were headed for landfill in China. Photo by Lightly.

Chrysalis by Lightly

PET:cell jewellery

by Tonya O'Hara

Photographs by Aiden d'Araujo

A fascination with the complexities of microscopic organisms and cells, along with concerns about consumption and pollution, inspired Tonya O'Hara to create a range of intricate jewellery with a pervasive waste material. Crafting by hand, she transforms reclaimed PET plastic drink bottles into rings, earrings, and bracelets in which an impression of fragility is contradicted by the durability of the material used.

\01: Lengths of nylon microfilament join clusters of small elements to create the *Jellyfish Chandelier* earrings.

Each form is developed through material experimentation, and no two pieces are exactly the same. The production process involves cutting each part by hand and shaping it with heat. The transparency of the plastic is retained, with the exception of the base of each ring formation, which is treated to take on a patina. Plastic rivets and nylon microfilament stems provide aesthetic consistency. Feather details are attached with silver crimps.

Tonya O'Hara (Leicester, UK) studied jewellery design at Birmingham Institute of Art and Design's School of Jewellery, and also at Loughborough University. Tonya's concerns for the health of the planet, her interest in componental design, and her fascination with transparency and microscopic organisms merged in her PET:cell range. She is hopeful of inspiring people to apply creativity and innovation to all aspects of their lives. Portrait by Aiden d'Araujo.

www.petcelljewellery.co.uk

PET:cell Jewellery by Tonya O'Hara

\02: The *Angel Wing* ring (left) incorporates feather details, while the *Apple* ring (right) combines two colours.

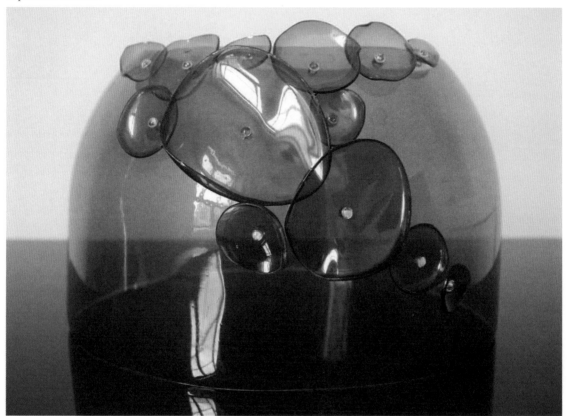

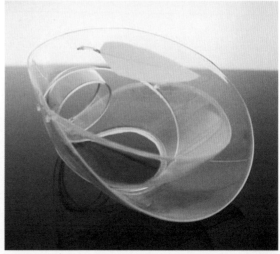

\03: The *Cellulose* bracelet (above) and the *Saturn I* and *II* rings (below) were inspired by the minute and immense worlds of cells and galaxies.

Particular PET bottles are selected for use based on their colour. Those used include sparkling mineral water, ginger ale, Coca-Cola, and Lucozade bottles.

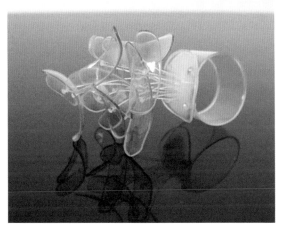 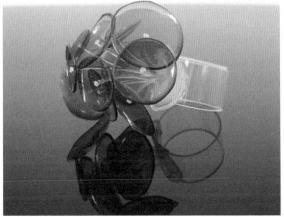

PET:cell Jewellery by Tonya O'Hara

\04: Clockwise from top left – the rings *Pear*, *Bobble*, *Quill*, and *Tarantula*.

bucket vase

by Qubus Design Studio / Jakub Berdych

Photographs by Gabriel Urbanek

For decades, the shape of the humble plastic bucket has remained unchanged. For sculptor and designer Jakub Berdych (director of Qubus Design Studio), this is a source of great fascination. He spent two years collecting buckets with the intention of using them in his creative pursuits. Inspiration struck when he observed the way flower shops display their stock without pretension in the simplest of buckets.

\01: The glass vase rests snugly inside the bucket and rises sculpturally above the rim.

The Bucket Vase combines a typical, mass-produced plastic bucket with a beautifully crafted blown glass vase. The contradiction was Jakub's intention. His aim was to establish a new relationship between the two parts, and transform one's perception of an ordinary object. The glass element can be used on its own, but its poetic impact relies on its coupling with a bucket. The Bucket Vase transforms the everyday into luxury.

Jakub Berdych (Prague, Czech Republic) established the Qubus design store with fellow designer Maxim Velcovsky in 2002 to present contemporary and conceptual Czech design products. Qubus Design Studio appeared in 2006, concentrating on commissions in interior, architectural, and graphic design. The gallery shop DOX by Qubus opened at Prague's DOX Centre for Contemporary Art in 2008. Portrait courtesy of Jakub Berdych.

www.qubus.cz

Bucket Vase by
Qubus Design Studio / Jakub Berdych

\02: The vases are made in two shapes and three shades of glass – yellow, black, and transparent.

reclaimed rooftile birdhouse

by t.n.a. Design Studio

Photographs by Héctor Serrano Studio unless otherwise stated

A witty combination of material, function, and embellishment links these bird habitats to their English context. The two birdhouses and the bird feeder were designed for common English garden birds. A reclaimed roof tile and pine boards (cut and engraved by laser) compose each miniature abode. The etched facades refer to the traditional English houses that the roof tiles would once have adorned.

\01: The bird feeder (left) and the small Victorian birdhouse (right) for wrens.

The habitats were designed by t.n.a. Design Studio for *TEN XYZ* – an exhibition shown by the UK design collective TEN. The exhibition explored various perspectives on sustainability issues within design that uses digital manufacturing technologies. When the designers discovered the high level of energy consumption by digital machines, they decided to optimise their use of the technology. Their use of the laser cutter allowed for the application of the decorative pattern at the same time as the cutting process.

Japanese-born designer Tomoko Azumi (London, UK) leads t.n.a. Design Studio and works in the fields of furniture, household and electrical products, lighting, exhibition design, commercial space design, and research. Tomoko trained as an architect in Kyoto and worked in a Tokyo architectural practice before studying furniture design at London's Royal College of Art. She established t.n.a. in 2005. Portrait by Julian Hawkins.

www.tnadesignstudio.co.uk

Reclaimed Rooftile Birdhouse by t n.a. Design Studio

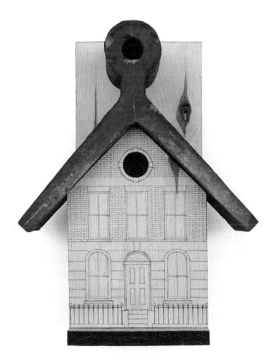

\02: The tall Georgian birdhouse (left) for blue tits and robins, and the small Victorian birdhouse (right) for wrens.

The use of digital machinery also influenced t.n.a.'s decision to incorporate reclaimed materials. The designers opted to exploit the flexible production capacity of the machinery to process the reclaimed materials, which tend to be irregular in shape and condition.

Right   Front   Left

Small Bird House X2   Large Bird House X1   Bird Feeder X2

Reclaimed Rooftile Birdhouse by
t.n.a. Design Studio

\04: Cardboard and paper prototypes in the studio, and a tile salvage yard. Photographs by t.n.a. Design Studio.

animal bud vase

by Studiomold

Photographs by Studiomold

A reclaimed sherry glass, a reclaimed plastic toy animal, and a plastic heat-shrink tube are the unusual set of components that constitute the ambiguous Animal Bud Vase. The random nature of the reclaimed elements makes each vase unique. The sherry glasses are reclaimed from pubs and restaurants and the toy animals are sourced from car boot sales and second-hand markets.

\01: Heat-shrink tubing is often used to insulate electrical wires. In this case, it transforms common objects into ambiguous new forms.

One might make out the impression of a sheep, a lion, a horse, a dinosaur, a giraffe, or a bison stretching through the all-encompassing white skin – a singular specimen of fauna to accompany a singular specimen of flora. A cat and a dinosaur are encased in the vases pictured here.

Studiomold (St Neots, UK) was created by Brendan Young and Vanessa Battaglia, who have been designing furniture and lighting together since 2003. Though they have expanded their portfolio to art direction, interior design, graphics, and communications design, the duo strives to remain faithful to their ideals about sustainable design. They recently founded a new company, Mineheart, for the production of "loveable design." Portrait by Studiomold.

www.studiomold.co.uk

Animal Bud Vase by Studiomold

While the sherry glass holds water, the upper part of the tube provides support for the flower's stem.

\02: Each vase stands approximately 170mm tall, and has a diameter of around 55mm.

colours

by Maria Cristina Bellucci

Photographs courtesy of Maria Cristina Bellucci

Jewellery designer Maria Cristina Bellucci loves to look at the materials that surround her in everyday life with fresh eyes, and to consider ways she might decontextualise the most familiar of items. Through her jewellery practice, she aims to give entirely new meanings to objects we use daily by making them unrecognisable in their new context.

\01: Three bulbs of colour and wood on a silver backing compose a brooch.

Her Colours range of rings, bracelets, brooches, and earrings is handcrafted with coloured pencils. She favours those with a hexagonal cross section as they fit together perfectly like the cells of a beehive, allowing her to form solid blocks. Once she has glued the pencils together, she works them as one piece of wood. She seals the final form by applying a non-toxic natural wax mixed with oils. It protects the wood and also makes it waterproof.

Maria Cristina Bellucci (Rome, Italy) developed a strong interest in jewellery after working for several years as a maker of costumes, accessories, and stage jewellery for theatre. While her early work was characterised by the use of very thin metal sheets and wires, recently she has explored more solid forms. Portrait courtesy of Maria Cristina Bellucci.

www.mcbjewellery.com

Colours by Maria Cristina Belluci

\02: Coconut wood forms a strong anchoring element in this large-format ring.

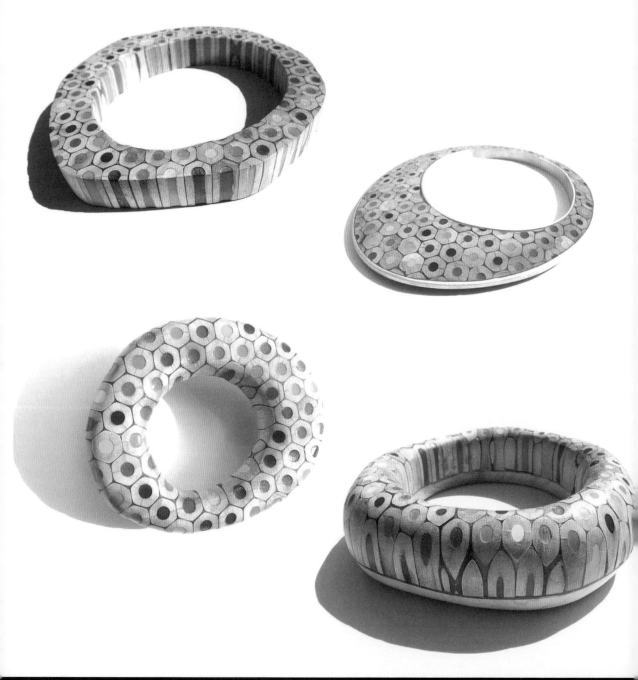

\03: Clusters of pencils stand alone or are combined with wood or silver to form a variety of bracelets and a brooch.

The irregular curvature of many of the thicker pieces results in changeable surfaces that morph from grids of perfect hexagons to warped swathes of colour and wood. Silver cases bring definition and strength to thinner pieces in the range, also concealing the pencils' unfamiliar inner profiles from view.

Colours by Maria Cristina Belluci

brick plan prototypes

by Rock Wang for Yii

Photographs by Rock Wang unless otherwise stated

The Dutch colonisation of Taiwan during the seventeenth century left an enduring legacy in the form of red-brick architecture. Used in contexts that have varied from palaces to farmhouses, Flemish-bond brickwork has become a familiar element of Taiwanese culture. The gradual loss of many old brick structures and the upgrading of others have begun to cause concern about a potential loss of cultural heritage.

\01: The undulating form of this tray provides a thoroughly contemporary translation of a historic material.

Designer Rock Wang devised a way to bring new life to old bricks and redefine the cultural significance of this common material for Taiwan. He collected chunks of brickwork from the ruins of an old house and transformed them into vases, bowls, and a sculptural tray – each with a style that belongs undeniably to the present day.

Rock Wang (Taipei, Taiwan) believes design should be pure and truthful. His approach is to find balance amidst conflict. He produced the Brick Plan Prototypes for Taiwanese design brand Yii – an initiative of the National Taiwan Craft Research Institute and the Taiwan Design Center. Yii translates the crafts and traditions of its country into the language of contemporary design. Portrait by Rock Wang.

www.yiidesign.com

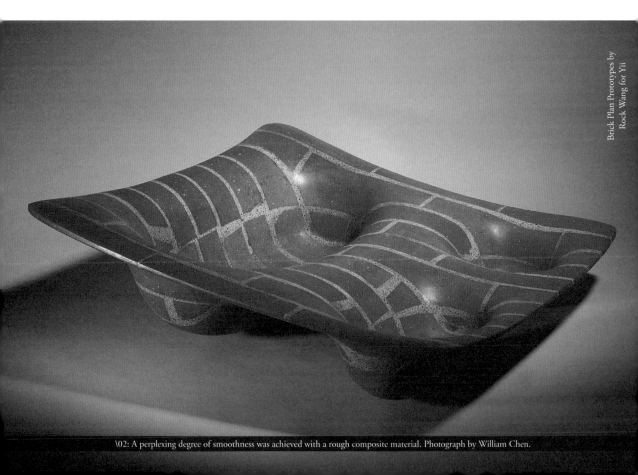

Brick Plan Prototypes by Rock Wang for Yii

\02: A perplexing degree of smoothness was achieved with a rough composite material. Photograph by William Chen.

Rock Wang collaborated with stone sculptor Pei-ze Chen and machinist Rui-Shan Huang during the production of the prototypes shown here. The undulating form of the tray was achieved with hand carving. The vases and bowls relied upon the use of machinery.

Interesting mortar patterns emerged after the reshaping of the brick blocks. The Flemish bond pattern could be discerned, along with irregularities in the material. Repetitive polishing achieved the surprisingly smooth finish of the pieces, which have provided a new translation of a historic element of Taiwanese culture.

Brick Plan Prototypes by Rock Wang for Yii

\04: Glimpses of the production process illustrate some of the labour involved.

BBQ bat house

by Stuart Haygarth

Photographs courtesy of Stuart Haygarth

The populations of birds, bats, and bees in urban areas of the UK have been experiencing rapid declines in numbers. To highlight this tendency, Phillips de Pury & Company (an auction house and art dealership) partnered with Adventure Ecology (an environmental awareness and travel initiative), and together they commissioned internationally renowned artists and designers to create bird, bat, and bee habitats.

\01: Designed for hanging, the dark habitat space can be entered from the underside.

The hand-made prototype habitats were produced with Phillips de Pury & Company's waste (such as cardboard, crates, invitations, catalogues, and plastics), and were auctioned in 2008 in London. The BBQ Bat House – a composition of black plastic sausage packaging trays – sold for £1,700. The proceeds from the auction benefitted the Sculpt the Future Foundation, which supports creative, innovative, and sustainable initiatives and promotes positive environmental change.

The work of designer Stuart Haygarth (London, UK) aims to give banal and overlooked objects a new significance. Since 2004, Stuart has been working on design projects that revolve around the collection of objects. He typically gathers objects in large quantities, categorises them, and assembles them in a way that transforms their meaning. Chandeliers, installations, and functional and sculptural objects are the result. Portrait courtesy of Stuart Haygarth.

www.stuarthaygarth.com

Habitats were also created by Jurgen Bey, Martino Gamper, Max Lamb, Tomoko Azumi, Peter Marigold, and others. All of the prototypes can be viewed in the "Auctions" section of Phillips de Pury & Company's website, www.phillipsdepury.com

BBQ Bat House by Stuart Haygarth

\02: Black-painted salvaged wood was used to build the structure and edge profile of the bat house.

02. furniture

bender stool

by Paul Evermann

Photographs by Matthias Ritzmann

Bender Stool invites the furniture user into the design process. The stool is succinctly divided into components – a powder-coated steel plate, zip ties, and three simple timber legs. Extensions of the round seat plate are bent twice to create open-format support casings for the legs. Zip ties hold the legs in place. Four more zip ties (pre-stressed and installed beneath the seat) provide structural tension and stability.

\01: The obvious expression of joints and the contrasts of materials and colours give each component a succinct expression.

Designed for sale in a flat-packed format, Bender Stool can be assembled easily without the use of tools. This, along with its ability to accommodate legs of various thicknesses, allows it to be customised by users to their tastes. Designer Paul Evermann's intention was to break with common ideas about design by involving unexpected elements such as found or used material.

Paul Evermann (Halle an der Saale, Germany) is a member of Designhaus Halle – a collective of young design professionals who work both independently and together. He studied industrial design at Burg Giebichenstein Kunsthochschule Halle, and interned at Atelier Haussmann in Berlin before starting his own practice. Portrait by Matthias Ritzmann.

www.paulevermann.com

Bender Stool by Paul Evermann

\02: This strong, stackable stool can be customised to the user's taste with found or used materials.

cabbage chair

by Nendo

Photographs by Masayuki Hayashi

Production of the pleated fabric with which Issey Miyake creates garments involves the simultaneous production of massive amounts of pleated paper, which is usually abandoned. The Japanese fashion designer invited design studio Nendo to make furniture with the paper for *XXIst Century Man* – an exhibition he was curating to commemorate the first anniversary of the gallery 21_21 Design Sight in Tokyo.

\01: The delicate 'peeling' of the chair takes around thirty minutes to complete.

In response, Nendo created the delicate and interactive Cabbage Chair – a many-layered roll of pleated paper that becomes a form of seating when the layers are peeled down. The transformation requires the outer layer to be cut, and the pre-cut inner layers to be folded down one at a time – a process that turns the furniture user into a craftsperson.

Oki Sato is the principal of multidisciplinary design studio Nendo (Tokyo, Japan). The studio, which has a second office in Milan, undertakes work ranging from architecture and interiors to events, graphics, furniture, and other products. With every project, the studio aims to create a "!" moment – a joyful response to an instance of richness and interest that illuminates our experience of the everyday. Portrait by Masayuki Hayashi.

www.nendo.jp

Cabbage Chair by Nendo

\02: The inner layers of the roll are narrower, and establish a backrest when folded down.

Astonishingly, the chair has no internal structure; the roll of paper alone can support the body's weight without collapsing. The sheer number of layers provides strength, but so too does the resin that is added to the paper during its initial production. The resin allows the paper to retain its pleated form, which results in a soft and springy sitting experience.

\03: The softness and delicacy of the chair suggests a gentle approach to its use.

Cabbage Chair by Nendo

The chair provides a subtle response to some of the issues that face designers in the twenty-first century, such as fabrication and distribution costs and environmental concerns.

\04: The forms of Issey Miyake's pleated garments are fully manifested by the wearers' bodies. Similarly, the chair requires completion by its user.

SCW

by Simon Ancher

Photographs by Simon Ancher

Being strong, sturdy, and lightweight, used plastic milk crates have long functioned as makeshift seating and storage solutions. As opposed to their intended storage function, they perform less ideally when overturned and used as seats due to the rigidity (and discomfort) of their plastic. Furniture designer Simon Ancher sought a way to increase comfort without altering or undermining the milk crate itself.

\01: SCW allows the portability and identity of the milk crate to be retained while seating comfort is greatly enhanced.

He devised a SCW (Stool Crate Wood) – a moulded plywood seating shell that 'melts' over the top of a standard milk crate. With the correct orientation of the milk crate preserved, a secondary storage function can also be enjoyed. The shells are handcrafted with a vacuum-forming technique, and a variety of laminates (in solid colours and timbers) are applied to the upper surface. SCW can also be used as a small table.

Simon Ancher (Launceston, Australia) is the program director of furniture design in the University of Tasmania's School of Architecture and Design. In addition, he runs Simon Ancher Studio, where he develops new products and undertakes commissioned pieces. During the development and production of SCW, Simon received technical assistance and manufacturing collaboration from Bruce Nye. Portrait by Simon Ancher.

www.simonancherstudio.com

SCW by Simon Ancher

\02: A central hole allows the shell to be easily picked up with one hand (by hooking a finger through and under the shell).

elasticshelf

by SystemDesignStudio

Photographs courtesy of SystemDesignStudio

The ElasticShelf was inspired by a project previously undertaken SystemDesignStudio, which incorporated rubber sheet material made from recycled tyres. The transformation of tyres into sheet material (such as that used for flooring) requires a time-consuming and costly process of shredding and gluing. The designers were keen to find a more direct way to reuse tyres.

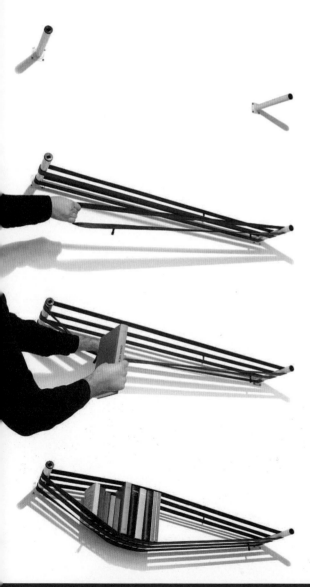

The used bicycle inner tubes were gathered from bicycle repair shops in Barcelona. The furniture legs were found at a collection centre for waste items that are to be recycled.

\01: The tension in the stretched tubes prevents the contained items from moving.

They hit upon the idea of an adaptable shelf system made with just two components: used bicycle inner tubes and the legs of discarded furniture. As its name suggests, the ElasticShelf utilises the elastic quality of the inner tubes to hold objects in place. Three tubes are simply stretched around two wall-mounted stems, which were cut from the legs of old office tables. The legs did not require painting, and their existing plastic end caps were also reused.

SystemDesignStudio (Barcelona, Spain) was established by architect Helbert Suarez and industrial designer Remi Melander. The studio works in areas of design ranging from architecture to daily objects, and always takes an experimental approach. The studio favours sustainable design concepts and endeavours to incorporate discarded objects, environmentally sensitive materials, and renewable energy into their projects. Portrait courtesy of SystemDesignStudio.

www.systemdesignstudio.com

ElasticShelf by SystemDesignStudio

tavolo cobogó

by Estúdio Campana for Plusdesign

Photographs copyright Plusdesign

Mid-century modern residential architecture took on a localised flavour in Brazil with the use of the cobogo. This perforated ceramic brick was incorporated into walls to allow breeze and sunlight to enter homes while visual privacy was maintained. Produced with a variety of decorative designs, the cobogo was named with the first two letters of the surnames of its creators – Coimbra, Boeckmann, and Góis.

\01: When used outdoors, the perforated tabletop allows the movement of the sun to be detected via intricate shadows.

True to their style of subversion and reinvention, designers Fernando and Humberto Campana conceived a new and surprising use for this familiar Brazilian building element. Transferring it from the vertical to the horizontal plane, the Campanas created a decorative table that casts patterned shadows on the ground. Cantilevered at the edges of the tabletop, the terracotta cobogo bricks are made to appear delicate and lightweight. A limited edition of the table was created for Italian gallery Plusdesign.

Brothers Fernando and Humberto Campana (São Paulo, Brazil) began working together in 1983, when Humberto asked Fernando to help him deliver a large order of handcrafted products. Though he graduated from law studies, Humberto had followed his passion for design and set up a small studio. Fernando graduated from architectural studies and was interested in alternative methods for design materialisation. They have since become well known for encouraging new perspectives of everyday objects. Portrait copyright Fernando Laszlo.

www.campanas.com.br

Tavolo Cobogó by
Estúdio Campana for Plusdesign

The Campana brothers have worked with scrap and disused material for many years. Their Favela Chair was designed in 1991, not long after their first exhibition. Production of this iconic scrap-wood chair began in 2003.

\02: Resin was used to bind the tabletop together. It reaches outwards like a canopy of leaves. The trunk-like legs are varnished steel.

drops pouffe and chair

by Camilla Hounsell Halvorsen

Photographs by Mads H. Palsrud

At the core of the bulbous Drops Pouffe and Chair are rubber inner tubes. These were reclaimed from used tyre stocks at car workshops. Nowadays, car tyres are typically sold in a tubeless format that minimises the risk of blowouts. Designer Camilla Hounsell Halvorsen redefined the disused inner tubes, giving them a new seating function by wrapping them with layers of scrap upholstery fabric.

\01: Bright and colourful fabrics were selected to reinforce memories of childhood craft activities – such as tassel making.

The design was inspired by the craft of tassel making, in which thread or yarn is wrapped around a medium (such as cardboard) before being snipped and tied together. Drops can be used as either a pouf or a chair thanks to a ring of stainless steel on its underside. The ring connects with the chair's under-frame – a steel ring with a slightly smaller diameter. One ring sits over the other, and the pouf can be tilted to the sitter's desired angle.

Camilla Hounsell Halvorsen (Oslo, Norway) recently completed a master's degree in interior architecture and furniture design at the Oslo National Academy of the Arts. Her master's design project involved the transformation of a 1920s mechanic's workshop building into a centre for contemporary craft. Camilla designed Drops while she was a student. Portrait courtesy of Oslo National Academy of the Arts.

www.camillahounsellhalvorsen.com

Drops Pouffe and Chair by
Camilla Hounsell Halvorsen

\02: In the chair format, rings of stainless steel allow the sitting angle to be adjusted.

mediaforce

by Ezri Tarazi
Photographs courtesy of Tarazi Studio

Israeli designer Ezri Tarazi recalls a childhood of filling sandbags, listening to cannons and shells, and finding a hole blown in the porch of his family's house. Today he is able to reflect upon how Israeli life involves a mixture of the military and the civic. This symbiotic connection takes many faces, he says – reserve duty for citizens, military slang used in everyday language, and domestic objects made from battle 'souvenirs' (for example, vases made from bomb shells).

\01: Like a protective armature, bars of iron surround and support the timber shelves.

Mediaforce is a cabinet inspired by these blurred distinctions. Made with used ammunition boxes and powder-coated iron, its design was influenced by the military equipment racks that hang on the sides of armoured vehicles. The timber powerfully communicates its past life via stencilled labels, bar codes, dents, scratches, and the evidence of straps and screws. It suggests that the home, too, is a military zone.

Ezri Tarazi (Shoham, Israel) is a professor at the Bezalel Art and Design Academy in Jerusalem. He headed the academy's industrial design department from 1996 to 2004, and founded the master's degree program (which he has since headed) in 2004. He founded the d-Vision internship program for young designers in 2005. Ezri is also an active designer, providing design services through Tarazi Studio. Portrait courtesy of Tarazi Studio.

www.tarazistudio.com

Mediaforce by Ezri Tarazi

Mediaforce was presented in Ezri Tarazi's 2011 exhibition *Kalab* at Paradigma Design Gallery in Tel Aviv. "Kalab" is army slang for "close to home." The exhibition explored notions of security, anxiety, and home.

\02: The past life of the timber can literally be read on the surface of the shelves.

cuisine d'objets

by 5.5 designers

Photographs courtesy of 5.5 designers

Meals often taste better when they are freshly made at home. Cuisine d'Objets presents a range of 'recipes' for furniture and lighting that can be homemade. A coat rack, a stool, a magazine holder, and a lamp are among the objects on the menu. The concept suggests that – as with diet – there is a link between the products we consume and our wellbeing (or sense thereof).

Cuisine d'Objets responds to today's context of economic uncertainty, as well as the decline in purchasing power faced by many consumers. But it also offers the satisfaction of personalised design input and the pleasure of making. What's more, it proposes an alternative to the seemingly endless industrial production of new objects. The authors of the concept, 5.5 designers, call it "gastronomy of a new era."

Vincent Baranger, Jean-Sébastien Blanc, Anthony Lebossé, and Claire Renard (Paris, France) established 5.5 designers in 2003. The group works with a commitment to conceptual rigour, and constantly questions their role and status as designers. Their quest for honest and accessible consumption alternatives lends a touch of humour to their work. They have designed products and environments for clients such as Centre Pompidou, Urban Outfitters, and Baccarat. Portrait courtesy of 5.5 designers.

www.cinqcinqdesigners.com

Cuisine d'Objets by 5.5 designers

\03: A length of timber (fitted with old hooks and handles) is set into a bucket, cooking pot, or bowl to make the coat rack.

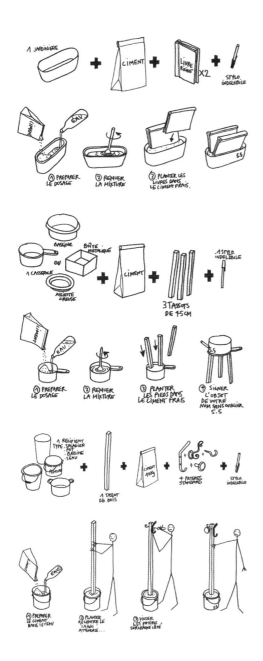

The designers' intention is to encourage the utilisation of whatever disused objects are at hand. Available for purchase, however, is a basic ingredient – a brass object that can be incorporated in order for the 'cooked' item to bear the designers' signature. In the case of the coat rack, the brass object is a hook; for the stool, it is a leg; and for the magazine rack, it is a handle-cum-vertical support.

Turn to page 272 to read more about Cuisine d'Objets, and how to make your own Cuisine d'Objets lamps.

Cuisine d'Objets by 5.5 designers

blockshelf

by Amy Hunting

Photographs courtesy of Amy Hunting

Amy Hunting's experiments with knotted cotton rope and blocks of waste timber resulted in Blockshelf – a customisable unit that can be readily dismantled and easily reassembled in alternate formats. Amy adopted knots that are traditionally used in sailing and fishing. Pulling the strings (by untying the knot at the bottom) allows the shelf to be dismantled. Reassembly is a playful process of restacking the blocks and shelves and retying the knot.

\01: The ropes hang from metal hooks. The ends of the rope are dipped in red wax – an indicator of handcrafting.

The blocks are collected from the waste bin of a London timber importer. More than twenty species of untreated wood are incorporated – a reflection of the variety of timbers available in the timber flooring industry (which is supplied by the importer). Blockshelf can be hung on the wall or from the ceiling, and thus it can also function as a room divider.

Norwegian-British designer Amy Hunting (London, UK) studied furniture and spatial design at The Danish Design School. She worked for Established & Sons before setting up her own practice in London. Along with developing and making furniture, Amy is a freelance illustrator. She enjoys seeking ways in which she can combine her passion for drawings and illustrations with furniture. Portrait courtesy of Amy Hunting.

www.amyhunting.com

Blockshelf by Amy Hunting

Amy Hunting is the co-founder and co-curator of Norwegian Prototypes (www.norwegianprototypes.com) – a collective of Norwegian designers who exhibit their work together in London.

\02: The irregularly shaped blocks emphasise the variability inherent in reclaimed waste materials.

pipe line bookcase

by Malafor

Photographs courtesy of Malafor

Offcuts of PVC sewerage pipe are a common by-product of house construction, and are often discarded. The design possibilities of this scrap material caught the attention of Polish designers Agata Kulik-Pomorska and Pawel Pomorski of Malafor. Its qualities, they decided, were ideal for furniture-making – it is strong, lightweight, easy to manipulate, and has a shape that encourages design experimentation.

\01: The outer surface and edge profiles of the pipes are painted while the inner surface is left white.

With seven short pieces of pipe and two straps, they created the Pipe Line Bookcase. This freestanding unit can be customised to any size by altering the number of pipes used. The buckled straps allow for adjustments. The round shelves are well suited to storing magazines, bottles, and books – but not precious knickknacks that require a flat display surface. Lightweight and easy to hold, the bookcase can be moved without difficulty.

Designers Agata Kulik-Pomorska and Pawel Pomorski (Gdansk, Poland) are partners in life and design. They established Malafor in 2004 after completing their industrial design studies at the Academy of Fine Arts in Gdansk. Malafor designs and manufactures furniture and objects whose form and shape are often surprising. The duo initiates their own projects and also takes commissions. Portrait courtesy of Malafor.

www.malafor.com

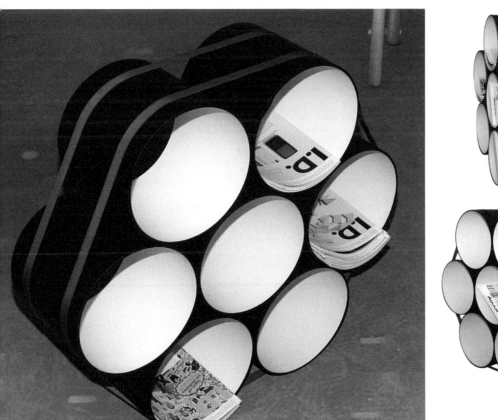

Pipe Line Bookcase by Malafor

\02: Contrasting red straps complete the two bold colour schemes, which complement the iconic nature of the bookshelf's form.

leg-acy

by Laurent Corio
Photographs by Laurent Corio

French designer Laurent Corio used a startlingly simple and direct gesture to thoroughly transform and redefine a traditional oak dinner table. He simply detached the four legs, sawed them lengthwise to double their number, and rejoined them in a trestle-leg fashion. Then he applied a glass top. An iconic old object was suddenly transformed into a new one that is just as memorable.

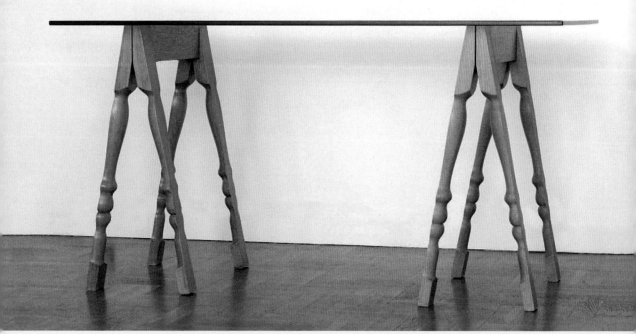

\01: Leg-acy asks questions (with some humour) about our time period. What do we do with the things we inherit?

Laurent explains his design with a short imaginary story about a teenager who inherits his grandmother's oak table. The youth decides to adapt the table to his more modern lifestyle without any concern for its historic value, and Leg-acy is the result. Laurent's underlying message is that consideration should always be given to the many issues associated with designing new objects and reusing older ones – value, identity, and sustainability among them.

Laurent Corio (Paris, France) set up his own design practice in 2008 after many years working for companies such as Moët Hennessy, Mugler Perfume, Jean-Paul Gaultier, Lalique, and Coca-Cola. He currently produces limited series and prototypes of objects, and does collaborative work with industrial and handicraft producers. He aims to design products in an honest way for companies that operate fairly, and break down boundaries between creative activities. Portrait courtesy of Laurent Corio.

www.laurent-corio.com

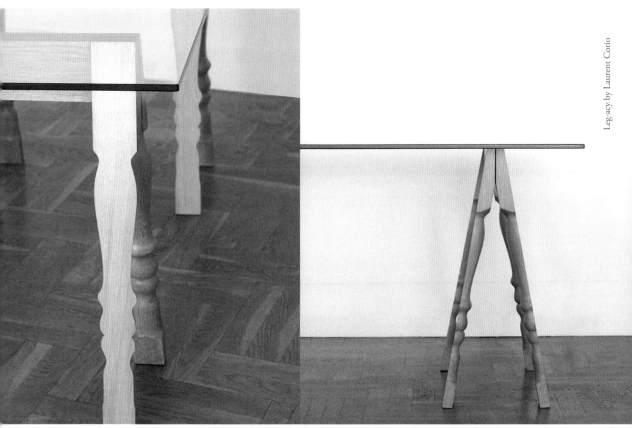

Leg-acy by Laurent Corio

\02: The ornate trestle legs create a memorable image. A transparent glass tabletop maximises the effect.

offcut

by Edwards Moore

Photographs by Edwards Moore

As part of Melbourne's State of Design Festival in 2010, an exhibition titled *Raising the Bar* was staged in a central city rooftop bar. The ten exhibiting architects were challenged to create the components of a working licensed bar using reclaimed materials and found objects. They produced seating, footstools, serving counters, lighting, and weather protection, and the exhibited items were utilised by bar patrons for the duration of the festival.

\01: The steel packing ties were painted black to emphasise colour contrasts. The seat is a tapestry of wood grains.

Offcut is a bar stool composed of lengths of reclaimed timber offcuts, which were gathered from building sites and dumpsters around Melbourne's inner suburbs. The pieces are held together in compression by a steel packing tie. Existing paint and other markings were intentionally exposed to lend each stool its own character. Gaps between the timbers at the sitting surface were filled with putty, and the stool was finished with linseed oil and wax.

Ben Edwards and Juliet Moore (Melbourne, Australia) explore a collaborative approach to architecture through their studio Edwards Moore. Although they are driven by a belief in the art of architecture as a global resource, they take cues from the essences of local culture. Place, time, and the social milieu inform their work, and every project is designed with environmental sustainability in mind. Portrait courtesy of Edwards Moore.

www.edwardsmoore.com

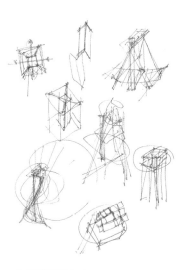

Offcut by Edwards Moore

The inspiration for the stool came from the tall, slender trees around Marysville – a town located 100km from Melbourne. The area was devastated by bushfires in 2009.

\02: The stool measures approximately 720 (h) x 280 (w) x 320 (d) mm, but the size varies according to the available timber.

trash cube

by Nicolas Le Moigne for Eternit

Photographs copyright Tonatiuh Ambrosetti and Daniela Droz

Strong and durable fibre cement is used widely in building construction – most often as a roofing material and for internal and external cladding. Swiss designer Nicolas Le Moigne collaborated with fibre cement manufacturer Eternit to create Trash Cubes – stools made with scraps of raw fibre cement that are left over from Eternit's production of building materials and products.

\01: Three hardened Trash Cubes sit behind a specimen that has just been removed from the mould for drying.

Measuring 310 x 310 x 360 millimetres, the compact stools were designed to have a basic form and to incorporate as many scraps as possible. Each stool goes through a metamorphic stage where the pliable raw material is condensed and sculpted in a box-like mould, and then hardened. While the overall shape remains consistent, the cubes are all unique. Their appearance varies according to how the scrap material settles.

Nicolas Le Moigne (Lausanne, Switzerland) graduated from ECAL/Ecole cantonale d'art de Lausanne, where he now teaches industrial design. He has also established his own studio. Nicolas has collaborated with companies including Eternit, Omega, Serralunga, and Pfister, and with galleries such as Gallery Libby Sellers, NextLevel Galerie, Helmrinderknecht Contemporary Design, and Galerie Ormond. Clarity and efficiency are qualities recognised in his designs. Portrait copyright Tonatiuh Ambrosetti and Daniela Droz.

www.nicolaslemoigne.com
www.eternit.ch

Trash Cube by
Nicolas Le Moigne for Eternit

\02: A smooth surface results where the fibre cement scraps touch the inside of the mould.

Nicolas' diagram describes the production process for the Trash Cubes: 01) Drop the scraps into the bottom of the mould. 02) Fill to three-quarters. 03) Place the curved open lid onto the top of the mould. 04) Continue to fill. 05) Fill to the brim of the mould. 06) Place the timber board on top. 07) Tap with a hammer to flatten the material. 08) Remove from the mould.

Although it is heavier than other materials that are typically used in furniture production, fibre cement offers good resistance to impacts and excellent durability.

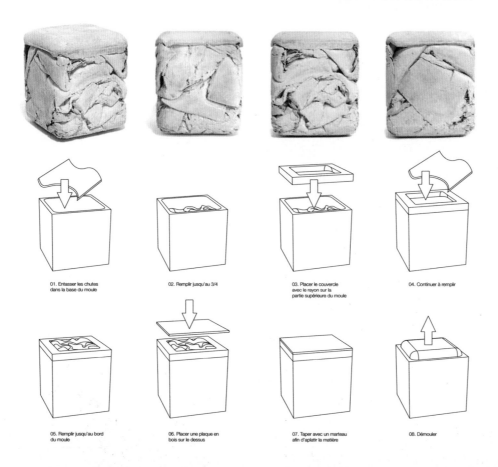

01. Entasser les chutes dans la base du moule

02. Remplir jusqu'au 3/4

03. Placer le couvercle avec le rayon sur la partie supérieure du moule

04. Continuer à remplir

05. Remplir jusqu'au bord du moule

06. Placer une plaque en bois sur le dessus

07. Taper avec un marteau afin d'aplatir la matière

08. Démouler

\03: The variability of the stools' surfaces is random, resulting from how the scraps fall into the mould.

Trash Cube by
Nicolas Le Moigne for Eternit

\04: Each stool remains in the mould for twenty-four hours before being removed for drying and hardening, which takes three weeks.

hey, chair, be a bookshelf!

by Studio Maarten Baas

Photographs by Maarten van Houten

A proportion of the goods that end up in second-hand stores cannot be sold due to damage or dilapidation, and need to be discarded. Always keen to experiment, Dutch designer Maarten Baas decided he would find a way to use these items. He collaborated with several second-hand stores in the region of Eindhoven and saved a variety of doomed objects from rubbish containers.

\01: These three-dimensional collages challenge our perception and reading of familiar forms.

He collaged furniture, lights, musical instruments, and other objects into seemingly chaotic assemblages. Each object gained a new function; for example, a chair became a bookshelf, a tuba became a vase, and a juicer became a hook. As the found objects were often weak, Maarten reinforced them with polyester and then coated them with polyurethane. Due to the unpredictable variety of available objects, every assemblage is unique.

Maarten Baas ('s Hertogenbosch, the Netherlands) approaches design without knowledge of, or care for, established boundaries. He simply experiments. His first product – a candleholder – went into production while he was still studying at the Design Academy Eindhoven. Today he works from a farm, where he also lives. His work ranges from charred chairs to cartoon-like porcelain tableware, and is not easily categorised. Many observers question whether it is art or design. Portrait by Frank Tielemans.

www.maartenbaas.com

Hey, chair, be a bookshelf! by Studio Maarten Baas

\02: The user of these unusual assemblages must interact with them to decipher the new suggested function of each component.

legged cabinets

by Ubico Studio

Photographs by Sahar Tamir

The work of Ubico Studio grows from a process of urban gathering and reclaiming. Materials are collected from dumpsters, renovation sites, and the streets of Tel Aviv, and used to create furniture and accessories (as well as interior spaces) that embody a sustainable agenda. Given equal importance is the notion of time and metamorphosis embedded in matter.

\01: The prototype (left), which incorporated a found drawer, provided the basis for the manufacture of refined versions (right) in batches.

The Legged Cabinets were conceptualised with a found drawer, which was cut angularly at its base and fitted with two readymade legs. With refinements to the proportions came the development of small and large versions of the prototype. These were made in batches with discarded materials including floorboards, doors, and offcuts of Corian. The waste materials were assembled to reflect the essence of the original drawer version.

Industrial designer Ori Ben-Zvi (Tel-Aviv, Israel) founded Ubico Studio in 2008. For ten years, Ori has been operating in the field of sustainable design as a practitioner and academic (at Holon Technology Institute). Ubico is a combined design studio and small production unit. The studio's aim is to generate high-quality design with good craftsmanship made solely of recycled and reclaimed materials. Ellia Nattel was a co-designer of the Legged Cabinets. Portrait by Sahar Tamir.

www.studioubico.com

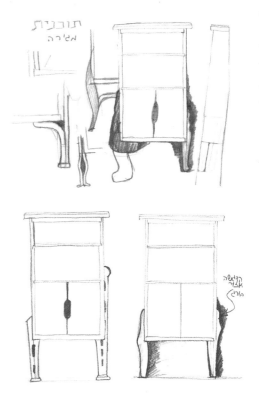

Legged Cabinets by Ubico Studio

\02: A larger cabinet was made with discarded pine doors, oak, reclaimed brass handles, and old plywood kitchen cabinet doors (with screen-printing).

stitch

by Studio Pepe Heykoop
Photographs by Annemarijne Bax

The reuse and reinvention of discarded or waste items implicitly suggests a degree of nurturing – of 'saving' and reinstating value. Dutch designer Pepe Heykoop took on a care-giving role when he upcycled a range of discarded chairs (and a lamp) that he found on the streets of Amsterdam and in second-hand shops. "We took care of them," he explained. And under the studio's care, the objects grew.

\01: Upholstery is given a thoroughly new meaning – one related to approximation rather than precision.

A loose skin of white cotton fabric was made for every object, and was hand-stitched in place. The skins were stuffed with soft fibres, and the objects became plump caricatures of themselves. The childish, comic-like quality was reinforced by the intentional irregularity of the black stitches, the mismatched buttons, and the waviness of the seams.

Designer Pepe Heykoop (Amsterdam, the Netherlands) often makes use of found objects and alternate materials to craft furniture, lights, and objects. Among other things, he has created a chair made with colourful toy blocks, an enormous inhabitable lampshade for a restaurant, seats made from stacked chairs that are bound with tape and wool, and a giant flexible lamp with an opening and closing shade. Pepe studied at the Design Academy Eindhoven. Portrait by Annemarijne Bax.

www.pepeheykoop.nl

Stitch by Studio Pepe Heykoop

\02: The upholstery has a levelling effect, rendering meaningless the style, features, and condition of the original furniture.

tatum's lounge

by Nine Stories Furniture Company

Photographs by Andrew Rumpler

While walking through a quiet neighbourhood in Brooklyn, New York, designer Andrew Rumpler (founder of Nine Stories Furniture Company) discovered a damaged upright piano in a debris container. Intrigued, he climbed into the container to take a closer look. After an hour or so, he left with what he felt were the most interesting parts of the instrument. Not coincidentally, these were also the parts knew he could carry back to his studio – the keys, wrapped in scrap paper and string.

\01: The ivory coating was stripped from the keys. Discs of resin safely seal in the remaining lead counterweights.

Andrew spent two years meditating on the keys, periodically unwrapping the package, studying the pieces, and laying them out in various formations on the floor of his studio. Each wooden key had a slightly different shape and length, and the lightweight basswood body of each key was proving a challenge to the creation of a load-bearing structure. Eventually, after much experimentation, a slender and surprising chair evolved.

Andrew Rumpler (New York, USA) founded the design/build studio Nine Stories Furniture Company in 1999. Central to the studio's practice is the process of making. This hands-on approach informs the ideas within furniture forms, as well as the final forms themselves. The studio values inventive problem solving over material worth, and aims to practice in a manner that achieves more with less.

www.ninestoriesfurniture.com

Tatum's Lounge by
Nine Stories Furniture Company

The bulk of an upright piano's keys are unseen from the keyboard. Tatum's Lounge incorporates the full length of the key lever.

\02: The seat, backrest, and rear leg join at the central apex, which is sheathed in an ultra-thin epoxy/glass matrix.

\03: Andrew uses resins as sparingly as possible. Tatum's Lounge contains about 25oz (around 700g) in the seat.

Tatum's Lounge was composed with twenty-five of the salvaged piano keys, and it weighs just six pounds (less than three kilograms). Each joint was cut by hand. The chair explores the structural limits of its components, and tests the faith of its occupant. A minimal cross-brace of metal rods provides the only additional support to the skeletal timber structure. The seat itself offers no further psychological reassurance – it is a mere skin of transparent epoxy casting resin.

The unlikely joining of elements and the play between balance and imbalance was inspired by the chair's namesake – revered American jazz pianist Arthur Tatum (1909–1956). "Tatum's Lounge," says Andrew, "requires of its occupant much the same commitment as the great pianist's music asks of its listeners – a certain amount of trust."

Tatum's Lounge by
Nine Stories Furniture Company

tis knot ottoman

by Lightly

Photographs by Cursor Ctrl

Almost one billion tyres for passenger cars, utility vehicles, trucks, and off-road vehicles are manufactured worldwide each year, reports The European Tyre Recycling Association (www.etra-eu.org). And every year, says the association, an almost equal number is permanently removed from vehicles and defined as waste. In Australia, thousands of tonnes of used tyres are sent to landfill or illegally dumped in bushland or waterways annually.

\01: Loose crocheting adorns the 'GTO' model. The landfill-bound tyres are thoroughly cleaned before being reborn as seats.

Australian design studio Lightly intercepts this flow of post-consumer waste. Tis Knot Ottoman features colourful heavy-duty nylon crocheted around used tyres, which are gathered from car yards and tyre shops. The crocheting involves a collaboration between designer Cindy-Lee Davies and knitter Sia Smyth. The aim of this occasional seating collection is to highlight the larger environmental issues at play in the creation and disposal of lifestyle consumer goods.

Cindy-Lee Davies (Melbourne, Australia) launched Lightly in 2005 in homage to her late grandmother. Her first products were homewares and lighting inspired by lace and doilies. The company now offers over eighty items that marry the aesthetics of traditional crafts with cutting-edge technology. Cindy-Lee's commitment to sustainable practice sees the bulk of Lightly products being made in Australia. Portrait by Cursor Ctrl.

www.lightly.com.au

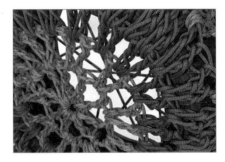

Tis Knot Ottoman by Lightly

Each style in the Tis Knot Ottoman collection is named after a car that was once (or still is) popular in Australia – for example, 'Torana,' 'Gemini,' and 'Datsun.'

replex table

by Oormerk

Photographs by Roel van de Laar

When we discard an old piece of furniture, we sacrifice the scents, shapes, memories, and crafting techniques that defined the object. These days, we all too often replace the discarded item with an anonymous, mass-produced one. Oormerk's development of Replex – an aggregate material containing fragments of timber from old furniture pieces – is a statement against this trend.

\01: By expressing the old in a new way, Replex Tables can be viewed as simultaneously fresh and familiar.

Initially, Replex was envisaged solely as a material. Clients could have a panel of Replex produced with parts of their own old furniture, and then use the panel as they pleased – in new furniture or as a wall panel, for example. The concept developed with Oormerk's decision to source its own supply of discarded furniture from recycling centres. The studio now produces its own series of Replex Tables.

Ruud van Hemert (right) and Stijn van Oorschot (left) established Oormerk (Breda, The Netherlands) as a design office and workshop. "Oormerk" is Dutch for "ear-tag" – an identification label often worn by cattle. Oormerk strives to develop a wide range of unique objects, but each bears the Oormerk identity. Ruud and Stijn are both designers and artists. They studied at the Academy of Art and Design St Joost in Breda. Portraits by Roel van de Laar.

www.oormerk.com

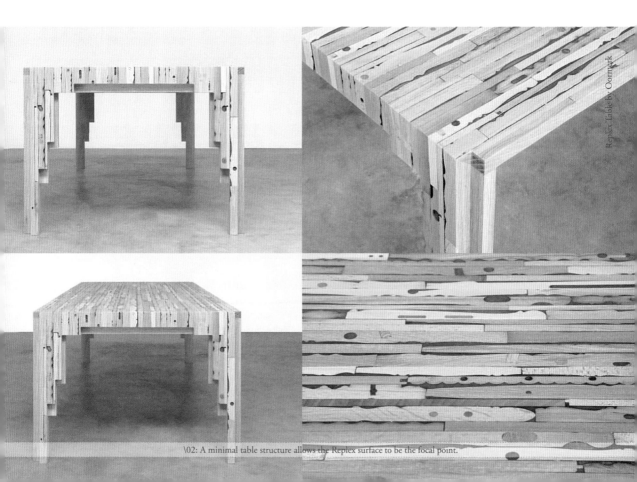

\02: A minimal table structure allows the Replex surface to be the focal point.

Replex Table by Oormerk

The Replex material is made with a process similar to veneering. Slices of old furniture are laminated onto thick timber base panels, which are made with discarded oak. The gaps are filled in with resin. Finally, a protective layer of hard wax or varnish is applied to protect the material. Familiar carved shapes stand out against the dark resin, and as such, memories are embodied and preserved in this new material.

\03: In this table, the Replex surface is expressed as a thin veneer that is barely visible at the edge of the tabletop.

Oormerk operates with a number of sustainable practice initiatives. Its transport and shipping is combined with other companies where possible. Its own transport is powered by propane gas. The office uses pdf documents and has neither a fax nor a photocopier. Recycled paper is used as part of corporate identity. Sawdust and unused furniture fragments are used for food smoking and in packaging for the automotive industry.

Replex Table by Oormerk

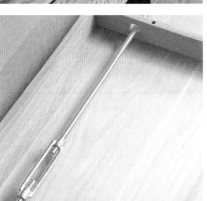

\04: Solid furniture becomes a thin veneer on thick timber base panels. Structural reinforcement is provided by tension rods.

honey i'm home

by Atelier Remy & Veenhuizen

Photographs courtesy of Atelier Remy & Veenhuizen

Tejo Remy and René Veenhuizen view everything in the world as a material that can be designed with. In their eyes, the things around them constitute an endless toolkit for design – the familiar can be memorably transformed and circumstances can be incorporated into designed objects. With this approach, the pair finds that they can thoroughly engage the users of their objects.

\01: With its apparently teetering components and complex structure, this cabinet (composed with parts of IKEA furniture) seems to be a chaotic stack.

Honey I'm Home is a stacking cabinet built with parts of old furniture and disused objects – glass bottles, flowerpots, files, and kitchen equipment. Many of these objects would once have sat upon a shelf. In becoming part of the cabinet itself, they dissolve the cabinet form. When it is filled with objects, the structural system of the cabinet is difficult to ascertain. The user's sense of disarray is compounded by the angles and cantilevers incorporated.

Tejo Remy and René Veenhuizen (Utrecht, The Netherlands) work together as product, interior, and public space designers. Their work explores the possibilities inherent in found goods and materials. They aim to create new meanings by using such objects and materials in alternate ways and contexts, thereby engaging the users of their objects on multiple levels.

www.remyveenhuizen.nl

Honey I'm Home by Atelier Remy & Veenhuizen

\02: When the cabinet is filled, one may wonder which parts are fixed and which can be removed.

heater chair and seat

by BorisLab

Furniture photographs by Francesco Ragusa
Action photographs by Christelle Collaud

A significant amount of metal – be it iron, aluminium, copper, or steel – comprises radiator heaters. Given the intrinsic value of such a mass of material, the discarding of radiators at the end of their functioning lives seems an absurdity. This impression struck designer Boris Dennler (founder of BorisLab) when he saw a beaten-up old radiator on a scrapheap. He said, "I got the idea of bashing up other old radiators to produce seats."

\01: A Heater Chair with legs sawn from an old stool (left) and a Heater Seat with repurposed metal tubes for support (right).

Each specimen of BorisLab's Heater furniture weighs between twenty-five and forty-five kilograms. His rudimentary production technique involves placing a radiator on two blocks and jumping on it. He then uses a ratchet lashing set to bend the metal further. The placement of wood offcuts between the radiator tubes controls the bending in the central area. Finally, he welds on legs reclaimed from old pieces of furniture and applies enamel paint. All pieces are numbered and signed.

Boris Dennler (Fribourg, Switzerland) likes to create objects that are radical (in terms of both form and material). He is deeply disturbed by the abundance of objects around him that seem doomed to obsolescence. He established BorisLab in 2004, and describes it as "a laboratory dedicated to the study of materials and shapes, to the valorisation of existing objects, as well as to gratuitous and improbable experimentation."

www.borislab.com

Heater Chair and Seat by BorisLab

\02: The bending process involves sheer physical force as well as gentler coercion using straps.

archeo collection

by Karton Art Design

Photographs by Pal Zakarias

Karton Art Design uses cardboard to breathe new life into old furniture that has fallen into disrepair. The Archeo line of one-off rejuvenated furniture was inspired by the restoration of ancient pots with new clay – specifically, by the way the new clay appears distinct from the original old fragments.

\01: The cardboard components that have been used to restore this buffet mirror the original parts while remaining distinctly 'other.'

Flat and monochromatic, the cardboard used to reconstruct each unique piece of Archeo furniture contrasts deliberately with the old carved timber components and their natural decorative grain patterns. It is a meeting of eras, techniques, aesthetics, and values. Karton Art Design also produces a range of flat-packed, collapsible cardboard shelving, which is fixed together with nothing but typical office clips.

Karton Art Design (Budapest, Hungary) is a two-person design studio. Installation artist Edit Szilvasy uses salvaged materials to create artworks, bringing new value to forgotten objects. Furniture designer Andras Balogh began his career as a cabinet-maker, and later obtained a degree in philosophy and sociology. The idea of creating cardboard furniture sprang from his interest in social issues and love for his craft. Portraits courtesy of Karton Art Design.

www.kartonart.eu

\02: Original carved elements are reinterpreted as arrangements of layered cardboard – like a geographical contour model.

Archeo Collection by Karton Art Design

bolt furniture

by Jamison Sellers

Photographs by Jamison Sellers

Dismayed by the material wastage that occurs in a throwaway culture, USA-based designer Jamison Sellers centres his practice on the use of reclaimed and salvaged materials. He developed his Bolt range to showcase the many beautiful species of domestic and exotic woods that can be found in salvaged shipping pallets. Each piece in the range features strips of planed pallet boards cut at 45-degree angles and arranged in an intricate pattern of contrasting colours.

\01: The door pulls on the Bolt Console were designed for unobtrusiveness using nails saved during the pallet disassembly.

The Bolt Console's pallet-wood doors are framed in a case made from locally sourced walnut. Salvaged nails serve as door pulls. The Bolt Desk (a commissioned piece) was produced entirely with salvaged pallets. The legs and frame elements are composed of three layers of half-inch-thick pallet boards. E1221 is an industrial-inspired table with a pallet-wood top and salvaged cast iron legs. Its name was derived by the only discernible markings on the legs.

Jamison Sellers (Providence, USA) studied furniture design at the Rhode Island School of Design. He focused his coursework on environmental studies – a move that helped him shape his practice in the realm of sustainable design. Through his work he aims to find and show the beauty that lies behind years of accumulated grime and dirt on a common component of global shipping activities. He produces his work at Keeseh Studio – a collaborative workshop space. Portrait by Elizabeth Moran.

www.jamisonsellers.com

\02: The console was designed for use in any room of the house. Internal shelves are adjustable.

Bolt Furniture by Jamison Sellers

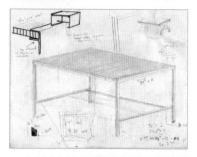

\03: The 1-in-thick top of the Bolt Desk is slightly offset above the base to create a floating appearance.

Bolt Furniture by Jamison Sellers

The Bolt range, which also includes a shelf and cutting boards, is finished with non-toxic, VOC-free natural linseed oil and varnish.

\04: In the E1221 table, the original 'bolt' pattern progressed into a vibrant arrangement of alternating arrows.

my family

by Sonia Verguet

Photographs by Sonia Verguet

Designer Sonia Verguet is ever curious about the offerings of flea markets. The experience of finding something that can no longer be purchased in stores, she says, is akin to finding treasure. Her preference for the many varied shapes of old, used objects has prompted her to incorporate found items into her design work. My Family is a collection of seats in which disparate flea market finds are united by a common new element.

\01: Pine boxes transform a group of disparate second-hand chairs and stools into a unified collection.

The shared gene that links stools, office chairs, rocking chairs, and dining chairs of various styles and ages is a plain timber box. The proportions of the box are varied to suit each particular set of chair components – the high back of a formal chair, or the petite legs of a low stool, for example. Sonia likens the seats to the members of a human family, seeing "tall uncles" and "small cousins" among their forms.

Sonia Verguet (Strasbourg, France) studied design at L'École Nationale Supérieure des Beaux Arts in Dijon and at L'École Nationale Supérieure des Arts Décoratifs in Strasbourg. Since 2009, she has worked as a professor of design and architecture at L'Institut Supérieur des Arts Appliqués. She also teaches 'food design' to children at a Strasbourg school. Her eclectic creative practice results in objects as diverse as furniture, suitcases, and cake pans. Portrait by Yohann Thomas.

www.soniaverguet.com

\02: The timber boxes establish a common seating condition, creating a play between consistency and variability.

My Family by Sonia Verguet

My Family was produced in collaboration with the contemporary art centre La Kunsthalle Mulhouse (located in Mulhouse, France) in 2010.

\04: The timber grains were aligned with a vertical orientation to conceal the joints in the new timber boxes.

latex roll pouf

by 13 Ricrea

Photographs by Francesco Arena

The work of Italian designers 13 Ricrea (which includes furniture as well as wall and floor coverings) does not begin with an exact and clear design concept. Rather, it is inspired by waste materials collected from factories – scraps of latex, felt, or plastic that are otherwise destined for landfill. The materials' characteristics are studied and explored, and ideas for designs grow organically from the inherent possibilities.

\01: The shoe-shaped cut-outs offer a constant reminder of the heritage of the material.

As its name suggests, the Latex Roll Pouf is essentially a roll of reclaimed industrial latex. The initial use of the latex – for the production of footwear insoles – can be easily read on these lightweight indoor seats. The material is well suited to a seating function due to its softness and cushioning quality. The colours of the seats depend on the latex available at the time of production.

Designers Cristina Merlo, Ingrid Taro, and Angela Mensi (Alessandria, Italy) established 13 Ricrea after thirteen meetings in 2007. The Italian word "ricrea" means "recreates" and the reinterpretation of material castoffs from industry is at the core of their practice. They work in the north of Italy, where the bulk of the country's manufacturing companies are based. Their location also allows transportation (and thus energy use) to be minimised. Portrait by Barbara Bartolone.

www.crearicrea.com

Latex Roll Pouf by 13 Ricrea

\02: The tightly wound rolls are fastened with plastic cable. The seat will readily mould to the user's body shape, ensuring comfort.

washed wood

by Cristina Covello

Photographs by Cristina Covello

Washed Wood is a series of furniture developed through a social design project, which aimed to create income streams for Brazilian craftspeople. Canadian designer Cristina Covello and Brazilian craftsman Zeca Godinho were connected by Brazilian facilitating organisation StraaT. Their collaboration produced stools, benches, coffee tables, and framed mirrors that combine traditional skills and materials with innovative techniques and a contemporary aesthetic.

\01: A stool and bench display the remnants of colourful paint, which reinforces the local flavour of the furniture.

The wood for the project was gathered from the demolished countryside shacks of sugar cane and coffee growers. The dirty painted boards required washing before use, and Zeca invented a machine that quickly cleaned them with motorised steel brushes. After cleaning, the wood was cut to lengths appropriate for each item of furniture. The strips were then cut to a precise width and angle that allowed them to be clamped together in a curve.

Cristina Covello (Vancouver, Canada) is a designer-maker who is interested in culture, craft, and how people use and relate to designed objects. She aims to tell a story with every object she designs, and spark a connection with the user. Equally important to her practice is the use of design principles that are sustainable in both environmental and social terms. Portrait courtesy of Cristina Covello.

www.cristinacovello.com

Washed Wood by Cristina Covello

This social design project aimed to alleviate poverty through a combination of craft and design. The prototypes were exhibited at a high-end gallery in São Paulo. This led to sales and additional custom work for craftsman Zeca Godinho.

\02: Zeca washed the reclaimed boards with his custom-designed machine (above right) before cutting and glueing them together (above left).

blow sofa

by Malafor

Photographs courtesy of Malafor

Dunnage bags are inflated volumes that are used to protect cargo during transportation. They are placed in the empty spaces between loads to provide stabilisation and cushioning. Waterproof and exceptionally strong, paper dunnage bags (composed of two layers of Kraft paper and one layer of plastic) can withstand pressure of up to two tonnes.

The Blow Sofa teams two reclaimed paper dunnage bags with a metal rack and rubber straps. Easy to transport when flat, and simple to inflate, the sofa has been designed for modern nomads and those who wish to minimise their material assets. The bags can be easily personalised with a pen, and they are inexpensive to replace should they become dirty. The sofa can be recycled at the end of its life.

Designers Agata Kulik-Pomorska and Pawel Pomorski (Gdansk, Poland) are partners in life and design. They established Malafor in 2004 after completing their industrial design studies at the Academy of Fine Arts in Gdansk. Malafor designs and manufactures furniture and objects whose form and shape are often surprising. The duo initiates their own projects and also takes commissions. Portrait courtesy of Malafor.

www.malafor.com

Blow Sofa by Malafor

sign stool

by Trent Jansen Studio

Photographs copyright Alex Kershaw

Exploiting the strength, durability, and graphic quality of used road signs, Trent Jansen Studio produces the Sign Stool 450 and the Limited Edition Sign Stool. The former was influenced by the base of an old steel drill press that occupied the workshop Trent used at the time of its design. Numbers, letters, lines, and colours are used as elements of design, and scuffs on the vibrant vinyl labels tell of the material's previous roadside existence.

Turn to page 50 to read about Trent Jansen Studio's Cycle Sign.

The Limited Edition Sign Stool involves a more complex folding arrangement to emphasise both sheet and volume. The folding of the metal at the ground plane does away with the need for rubber feet, minimising the use of resources. Graphic elements are displayed both externally and internally. Offcuts created during the manufacture of the Sign Stools are used by the studio to produce Cycle Sign – a reflector disc for bicycles.

After completing his studies at the College of Fine Arts, University of New South Wales in 2004, Trent Jansen (Sydney, Australia) interned at Marcel Wanders' Amsterdam studio. Trent established his own studio after returning to Australia later that year. His key aim is to practice "honest and poetic sustainable design" by developing objects of longevity that will maintain a lasting relationship with their users. Trent has also held teaching posts at several Australian universities. Portrait copyright Tobias Titz.

www.trentjansen.com

Sign Stool by Trent Jansen Studio

\02: The more playful Limited Edition Sign Stool was produced in a run of only fifty pieces.

new and improved

by Chromoly

Photographs by Shanghoon

"If you're going to change something, why not make it better?" asks Canadian design studio Chromoly. In the New and Improved range of furniture, Chromoly questions the conventional understanding of repair – that it involves restoring things to their previous state. Rather, Chromoly alters damaged wooden furniture by replacing its broken or missing parts with bronze replications of the original parts.

\01: The bronze parts are cast in moulds of the existing timber forms. As such, grain patterns can be read on the bronze.

What were once the weakest parts of the furniture become the most permanent and precious. The relationship of the broken parts to the whole is reversed. To enhance the visual contrast between the new and existing parts, the timber is uniformly stained to an ebony shade. As though the furniture has been grafted, the reflective bronze and the dark timber are snugly united along precise seams.

Chromoly (Toronto, Canada) is a creative studio founded by art director Adam Pickard and product designer Jonathan Sabine. While Jonathan gravitates towards the practical and well rounded, Adam produces work that is clever and unexpected. They both, however, appreciate the pursuit of purity in ideas and form. Adam has worked with advertising agencies around North America and Europe. When Jonathan is not working on Chromoly projects, he develops designs for his studio Mat Cult.

www.chromoly.ca

New and Improved by Chromoly

\02: The amount of bronze used was optimised; apparently solid parts are simply shells.

The appearance of the furniture will change over time as the surfaces of the bronze parts oxidise.

\03: Intermittent studs on the perimeter of the existing tabletop were replicated in bronze.

New and Improved by Chromoly

\04: A chair, side table, and coat rack have been produced. The consistent material expression unites the variant forms.

bookfor armchair

by Fordesignfor

Photographs courtesy of Serena Riccardi

The story of the Bookfor Armchair is one that can be co-written by its users. This interactive piece of furniture contains 'pages' of fabric that can be flipped, removed, or replaced. The seat and back of the chair are composed of layers of textile – either various remnants recovered from diverse sources, or neatly folded pieces of fabric made from certified organic fibres. 'Pages' can be removed or added with the turn of a screw.

\01: The degree of cushioning provided by the chair can be customised. Its colour and style can be personalised.

The frame of the chair is constructed with steel reinforcing bars (rebars) recovered from concrete structures. The rebars are bent and welded to form an angular frame. Steel mesh provides support for the seat and back. Upon this base structure, the Bookfor Armchair can be 'written' with many styles, textures, and colours of fabric (or other materials). The rubber tips from recycled walking sticks provide grips for the chair's feet.

Industrial designer Luca Gnizio (Milan, Italy) established Fordesignfor in 2007 with the aim of transforming recovered materials into furniture. He seeks ways to turn objects and materials discarded by factories and industry in general into desirable and functional designs that will enrich daily life. Prior to establishing his own brand, Luca created prototypes for large companies, and also worked in the fields of interior and packaging design. Portrait courtesy of Serena Riccardi.

www.fordesignfor.com

Bookfor Armchair by Fordesignfor

\02: The steel reinforcing bar is not painted or treated. This contributes to the impression of a chair constantly 'in progress.'

hk table

by &Larry

Photographs courtesy of &Larry

Singapore's eclectic HongKong Street straddles the city's central business district and the Chinatown enclave. It accommodates businesses that range from old-time foodstuff traders to architecture studios. Walking along the street daily, designer Larry Peh noticed the abundance of packing crates discarded by the food traders. He recongised an opportunity to reuse them for the construction of a functional work of art.

\01: A glass top is supported by a structure of two packing crates and additional lumbar (connected with brackets and screws).

The handcrafted HK Table offers an expression of the volume contained by a packing crate as well as the thinness of its components. The table was designed to pay tribute to the mercantile industriousness of HongKong Street, while bringing a higher level of appreciation to a humble utilitarian object. It is an object that speaks of identity to a Singaporean audience, while also offering relevance to a wider group.

&Larry (Singapore) is a creative studio that believes art and design should not exist in vacuums. Directed by Larry Peh, the studio undertakes a diverse body of work that ranges from posters and print campaigns to a series of Singapore-inspired art objects. A spirit of collaboration and mutual respect is fostered in the studio, and this extends from the personal level to the wider social and physical environments. Portrait courtesy of &Larry.

www.andlarry.com

HK Table by &Larry

\02: An abundance of crates are discarded at the roadside along HongKong Street.

neorustica

by Jahara Studio

Photographs courtesy of Jahara Studio

Neorustica is a collection of cabinets, tables, and benches constructed with scrap wood in Brazil. Each of the ten pieces in the collection is named after a shantytown or favela in Rio de Janeiro – the hometown of the designer, Brunno Jahara. He wished to pay homage to the country's rural background and highlight the living conditions endured by many who move from the country to the city.

\01: The cabinet interiors are lined with a special laminate made from recycled PET bottles. The surface is durable and easy to clean.

As such, an improvised character pervades the Neorustica range. Brunno collaborated with a furniture manufacturer that specialises in working with scrap wood from construction and demolition sites. Rough wood slats were painted with bright, contrasting colours and assembled into panels and doors. Water-based paints and non-toxic varnish were used. The roughness of the aged wood invites users to touch the furniture and feel its texture.

The work of designer Brunno Jahara (São Paulo, Brazil) is globally and locally inspired, and represents his own Brazilian background as well as his interpretations of our multicultural world. After his studies, Brunno worked at Fabrica's Design Department. Now with his own studio, he works across diverse media including but not limited to graphic applications, furniture, installations, retail interiors, and jewellery. Portrait by Paola Bellani.

www.jaharastudio.com

Neorustica by Jahara Studio

\02: Named after various favelas and inviting interaction, the pieces encourage a similarly open attitude towards Rio de Janeiro's poorest quarters.

rubens collection

by Frank Willems

Photographs by Serge Hagemeier, Masha Matijevic, and Frank Willems

A visit to a Dutch waste processing facility alerted designer Frank Willems to the fact that the lives of most household items – cupboards, chairs, tables, and so on – can be readily extended. An exception, however, is mattresses. They appear to have no destination other than landfill. Frank dedicated his thoughts to finding a way to reuse mattresses in a hygienic fashion.

\01: In Plus de Madam Rubens, the folded mattress forms a comfortable, voluminous seat on top of an antique chair frame.

The result is the quirky Rubens Collection – a colourful range of plump furniture that incorporates folded and painted foam mattresses. The paint creates a hygienic coating and refreshes the foam. Several seating styles populate the collection – Madam Rubens (in which the folded mattress is attached to the frame of a reclaimed stool), Petit Pouf (essentially a folded bundle of foam), and Plus de Madam Rubens (integrating a reused chair).

Frank Willems (Eindhoven, The Netherlands) has a passion for adventure. He initially trained in advertising and presentation techniques, but further studies at the Design Academy Einhoven have sent him on a trajectory of three-dimensional design. Frank does not consider himself to be dedicated to 'green' design; rather, his tendency is to bring unrelated ordinary objects together. Portrait by Irmgard Geelen.

www.frankwillems.net

Rubens Collection by Frank Willems

\02: The folded mattress is held in place and attached to the chair frame with straps, which are also painted.

\03: Madam Rubens (above) and Petit Pouf (below). The compact and asymmetrical folding styles are illustrated.

Frank folds the single-bed mattresses in two ways. Compact folding creates a narrower but taller foam bundle. Asymmetrical folding creates a wider bundle with less height. The use of found stools and chairs results in a virtually endless variety of leg profiles for the two Madam styles.

Each year, reports designer Frank Willems, Europeans throw away 12 million cupboards, 3 million kitchens, 21 millions chairs, 7.2 million tables, and 18.4 million mattresses.

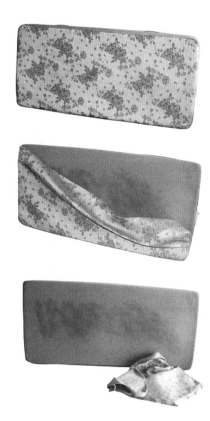

Rubens Collection by Frank Willems

treasure furniture

by Studio Maarten Baas

Photographs by Maarten van Houten

What qualities and characteristics make something a treasure? The value of the material with which it is made? Its uniqueness? A sacred purpose, or the symbolism of its form? Its rediscovery after being lost and forgotten? The Treasure Furniture designed by Maarten Baas offers both conventional and unconventional interpretations of notions of preciousness. It was made with waste from a furniture factory – specifically, with offcuts of inexpensive MDF.

\01: Twenty-three Treasure armchairs were created, with red felt or black leather upholstery and a black-painted MDF frame.

As the furniture produced in the factory is replicated, so too are the waste offcuts. This made it possible for Maarten to reproduce the Treasure Furniture. He created a limited-edition batch using the readily available fibreboard. The forms he designed echo standard seating shapes, yet they express an abstract, makeshift aesthetic particular to Maarten's vision. They are an expression of the potential value of inexpensive scrap material – even when it is abundant.

Maarten Baas ('s Hertogenbosch, the Netherlands) approaches design without knowledge of, or care for, established boundaries. He simply experiments. His first product – a candleholder – went into production while he was still studying at the Design Academy Eindhoven. Today he works from a farm, where he also lives. His work ranges from charred chairs to cartoon-like porcelain tableware, and is not easily categorised. Many observers question whether it is art or design. Portrait by Frank Tielemans.

www.maartenbaas.com

Treasure Furniture by Studio Maarten Baas

\02: Fifty-eight Treasure dining chairs were constructed and painted black, white, or yellow.

pied de biche

by Peter Marigold

Photographs copyright Gallery Libby Sellers

Pied de Biche fuses two polar methods of furniture production – mass manufacture and handcrafting. It was made with second-hand standardised industrial steel shelving components. Its feet, however, were cut and re-welded in a traditional pied-de-biche form. Nothing was added to the metal; the form was simply forged from the material itself via an explorative process of designing through making.

The French term "pied-de-biche" refers to a type of furniture leg with a slight curve, ending in a form that resembles a cloven hoof.

\01: The intentional disjunction of the legs highlights the potential for standardised forms to be altered and redefined.

The piece was inspired by a visit to a scrap yard where designer Peter Marigold saw a pile of rusting, decaying metal shelving. "I felt that these forms were interesting in relation to the evidence that material is not concrete, but ever changing," he explained. While highlighting the transformative quality of material, Pied de Biche also questions the fixed nature of standardised forms. Peter produced twelve shelves in a limited edition series for Gallery Libby Sellers in London.

Peter Marigold (London, UK) is a sculptor-turned-furniture designer. He approaches furniture design as a formal sculptural activity, working directly with materials. His pluralistic and resourceful approach often sees him finding DIY solutions to design challenges. He established his workshop and studio in 2006, and produces work for private commissions, mass production, and galleries. Peter studied art and sculpture at Central St Martins College of Art and Design, and design products at the Royal College of Art. Portrait courtesy of Peter Marigold.

www.petermarigold.com

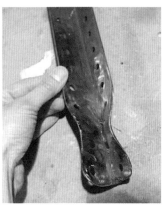

Pied de Biche by Peter Marigold

\02: After a quick paper model, a metal prototype was made to test the form.

banco machado

by Mônica Rodrigues Fernandes / Vértices Casa

Photographs by Mozart Fernandes

Designer Mônica Rodrigues Fernandes created Banco Machado to highlight an issue that often surrounds products made with reclaimed materials – the fact that customised design and manufacture using skilled labour will generally result in an object of higher cost (and value) than a less sustainable, mass-produced counterpart. She fears that many people who opt for cheaper, factory-made objects may not consider the consequences of doing so.

\01: The depth of the cut lends the structure an air of precariousness.

Banco Machado is constructed with layers of waste timber that would otherwise be discarded from lumbar sheds. An image of human (rather than factory) production is expressed with an angular void that is shaped as though it has been cut by an axe. It deeply penetrates the cube form, pushing the stool to its structural limit. It is a statement of the versatility of timber and of the possibilities of human experimentation.

Prior to establishing design studio and store Vértices Casa with her partner Mozart Fernandes, Mônica Rodrigues Fernandes (São Paulo, Brazil) worked in the film industry doing production as well as acting. Vértices Casa creates scenography, props, and mobile spaces – often with reclaimed wood found in dumpsters. The store also sells the work of a number of Brazilian creatives. Mônica practices photography as a hobby, capturing urban scenes in São Paulo. Portrait by Mozart Fernandes.

www.verticescasa.com.br

Banco Machado by
Mônica Rodrigues Fernandes / Vértices Casa

deckstool

by Podlaski Design

Photographs courtesy of Podlaski Design

Skateboard artwork enjoys a second coming on Deckstool – a compact piece of furniture made from broken and discarded skateboard decks. The shape of the stool was informed by the consistent pattern of breakage displayed in a number of boards. The designers also wished to use the waste efficiently to create a repeatable product that could be manufactured in high numbers.

\01: Scuffs and scrapes are celebrated as a layer of patterning on the artwork.

The stool's components are interchangeable but every stool exhibits its own unique features thanks to the variability that exists in skateboards – in particular the differences in artwork, the different colours in their plywood, incidental graffiti, personal decorations, or damage caused by the original owner of the board. Repurposed metal skateboard hardware is used to join the deck elements.

Jason Podlaski (Philadelphia, USA – pictured above right) is an industrial designer and entrepreneur with varied experience in the furniture and architectural industries. He established Podlaski Design in 2005. His brother Adam (pictured above left) provided the catalyst for the development of Deckstool when he asked Jason to collaborate on the design of a piece of furniture using his pile of old broken decks. Portraits courtesy of Podlaski Design.

www.deckstool.com

Deckstool by Podlaski Design

\02: The metal 'trucks' and axles that connect skateboard wheels and decks join the parts of each stool.

ricrea outdoor collection

by 13 Ricrea

Photographs by Francesco Arena,
Barbara Bartolone, and Ingrid Taro

For the creation of its furniture and furnishings, 13 Ricrea dedicatedly makes use of scrap materials from the factories of northern Italy. The designers allow the waste materials to guide their design conceptualisation, design development, crafting, and packaging. Their philosophy is a holistic one; they have also extended their activities to social rehabilitation, working with service providers on projects with common aims.

\01: Various forms of seating and vases compose the collection. Hanging overhead (to provide shade) are offcuts of felt.

The Ricrea Outdoor Collection contains various chairs, benches, poufs, and vases made with petals of reclaimed plastic sheet. The waste material is leftover from the manufacture of lifeboats and other inflatable vessels, and thus is perfectly suited to outdoor use. Each petal is cut by hand and stapled to the frame. The frames are made with materials such as used tyres and reclaimed timber.

Designers Cristina Merlo, Ingrid Taro, and Angela Mensi (Alessandria, Italy) established 13 Ricrea after thirteen meetings in 2007. The Italian word "ricrea" means "recreates" and the reinterpretation of material castoffs from industry is at the core of their practice. They work in the north of Italy, where the bulk of the country's manufacturing companies are based. Their location also allows transportation (and thus energy use) to be minimised. Portrait by Barbara Bartolone.

www.creatricrea.com

Ricrea Outdoor Collection by 13 Ricrea

Turn to page 158 to read about 13 Ricrea's Latex Roll Pouf – an indoor seat made with latex waste from the production of insoles for footwear.

\02: A bench, chair, and vases indicate the variety of forms that can be produced with the versatile material.

keep

by Petter Thörne and Anders Johnsson for Muuto

Photographs by Gils Photography and Ibsen & Co

The potential of waste materials to bring uniqueness to a design, as well as a narrative of the past, inspired Petter Thörne and Anders Johnsson to experiment with scrap timber. The designers were keen to show that when used in the right context, waste materials can produce objects that offer equal appeal to those made with new materials. They developed Keep – a limited-edition dining table produced by Muuto.

\01: A sense of ordered randomness was achieved with the variety of scrap timbers. Each table is different.

The majority of the waste material was collected from carpenters in the Swedish city of Jönköping, where the tables were made. Petter and Anders also collected useful materials during travels to Copenhagen, Hamburg, and London, and some of these have been incorporated. The lengths of scrap timber were assembled into a rectilinear structural frame and held together with black metal bands. The carpenter was Martin Almberger.

Petter Thörne (London, UK – left) and Anders Johnsson (Stockholm, Sweden – right) met at Konstfack School of Design in Stockholm. Their work aims to challenge standards and habits, investigating the emotions and people that lay behind design. In parallel to their collaborative work, Anders works with Strategisk Arkitektur in Stockholm and Petter studies at the Royal College of Art in London. Muuto is a Scandinavian design company founded in 2006 with the goal of reinvigorating Nordic design. Portraits courtesy of Petter Thörne and Anders Johnsson.

www.andersjohnsson.se
www.petterthorne.se
www.muuto.com

Keep by Petter Thörne and Anders Johnsson for Muuto

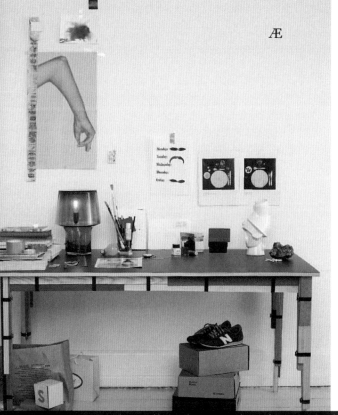

Æ

Keep was the first winner of Muuto's student design competition (the Muuto Talent Award). The jury liked the responsible concept, its character, and its Scandinavian references. The table came into production and was launched in 2010.

\02: The tapered legs reach a surprising degree of thinness at their feet. A dark laminated tabletop unites the composition.

tannin lounger

by Kieran Ball

Photographs by James Field

During a tour of a tequila distillery in Mexico, Australian designer Kieran Ball was struck by the idea of using spent oak barrels to produce high-end furniture. At the time, he was working on a line of sustainable furniture as part of an internship with Mexican design firm EzequielFarca. He began experimenting with how he could manipulate the used timber from tequila barrels, resulting in an initial concept for the Tannin Lounger.

\01: The slim structural frame of steel is subtly revealed at the long edges of the lounge.

Back in Australia, Kieran developed the idea further using locally sourced wine barrels and produced the first Tannin Lounger. It combines slices of oak with a curving stainless steel frame. The oak slats resulted from the sectional cutting of barrel staves, and they reveal the curved side profile of the original barrel. This technique allowed nearly ninety-five per cent of the barrel to be used. It also subtly revealed the timber's story, with wine staining evident along one edge of every slat.

Kieran Ball (Adelaide, Australia) graduated from the University of South Australia's industrial design course after working as a junior designer at EzequielFarca in Mexico City. He developed the Tannin Lounger during his final year of study. Kieran enjoys the adventure that accompanies working with reclaimed materials. He finds that (as opposed to virgin or custom materials) a reclaimed material will drive a design towards a solution that might not otherwise have been considered. Portrait courtesy of Kieran Ball.

www.kieranballdesign.com.au
www.ezequielfarca.com

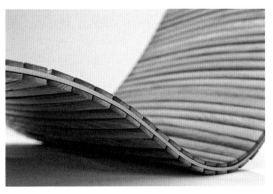

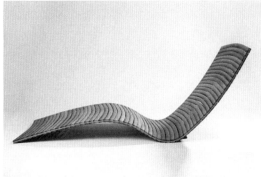

Tannin Lounger by Kieran Ball

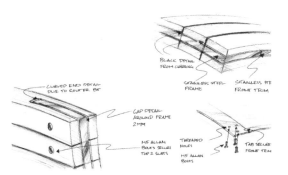

The timber used for constructing wine and spirit barrels is sourced from American or French Oak trees that are often over 100 years old, says designer Kieran Ball, yet the average life of the wine or spirit barrel is just five-to-seven years.

lived wood

by Tom Thiel

Photographs by Tom Thiel (VG Bild)

The undulating surfaces of Tom Thiel's furniture may lead one to question whether these specimens are artworks or functional objects. Tom describes his work as something between fine art and industrial design. Purely autonomous artworks, he asserts, would be restored if traces of use appeared. Rather, he creates a new functional context for materials that are charged with narratives of use and a sense of time.

\01: The Complicated Table took more than a year to build. It contains over 1,000 pieces of scrap wood and weighs 140kg.

As such, Tom makes possible a continued accumulation of meaning through use. He works mostly with wood that he finds on the streets or in buildings that are about to be demolished. With simple tools and techniques, he removes any 'disturbing' elements such as dirt, protruding nails, unattractive layers of paint, or splintered areas. He allows some old traces to remain and tell their story, and adds traces of his own.

Tom Thiel (Hamburg, Germany) has been working with salvaged wood for over fifteen years. He studied at the University of Art in Kassel, and later undertook architectural studies at the University of Applied Sciences in Hamburg. He draws inspiration about transient beauty and the value of used objects from *wabi sabi* philosophy and African tribal art. His accumulative furniture is made with simple crafting techniques that will allow for easy repairs in the future. Portrait by Ulrich Kellermann.

www.gelebtesholz.de

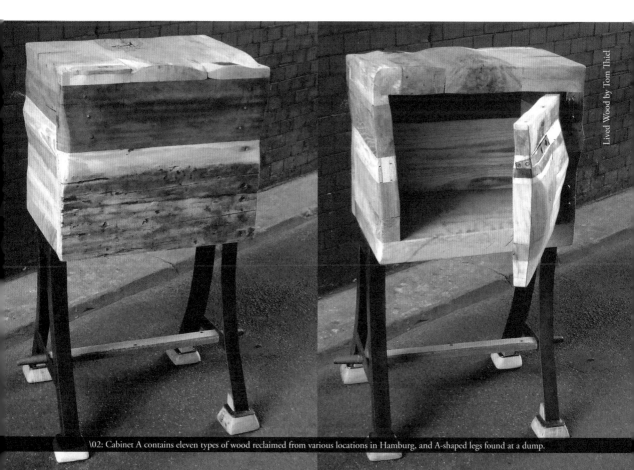

Lived Wood by Tom Thiel

\02: Cabinet A contains eleven types of wood reclaimed from various locations in Hamburg, and A-shaped legs found at a dump.

about waste

by Filipa Ricardo

Photographs courtesy of Filipa Ricardo

Scrap plywood produced during an industrial process is combined with unwanted blankets to create this unique stool. About Waste sandwiches layers of colourful reclaimed woollen blankets (sourced from second-hand stores in Eindhoven, the Netherlands) between two panels cut from a 'sacrificial board' – a timber substrate used with CNC routing equipment.

\01: The character of the materials used to make the stool is unpredictable. Photograph by Ivano Salonia.

A sacrificial board allows a router to penetrate the work piece without damaging the base of the machine, and is typically discarded after use. The unique random patterns engraved onto such boards captured the attention of designer Filipa Ricardo. She teamed them with steel rods and granted them a new purpose as part of the rigid structure of About Waste. This project was the result of a residency at the MU art space in Eindhoven.

Filipa Ricardo (Lisbon, Portugal) completed her industrial design studies at ESAD (Escola Superior de Artes e Design) in Caldas da Rainha, Portugal, and then ventured to the Netherlands. There, she undertook an internship and an artistic residency under the wing of MU in Eindhoven. Since returning to Portugal, she has been developing projects as a member of the design group Colectivo da Rainha. She also works as a freelance product designer, taking commissions from companies and organisations. Portrait courtesy of Filipa Ricardo.

www.filiparicardo.com
www.colectivodarainha.com

About Waste by Filipa Ricardo

\02: Either end of the stool can be sat upon. It can also be produced in a bench format. Photograph on the left by Ivano Salonia.

patchwork furniture

by Amy Hunting

Photographs courtesy of Amy Hunting

Amy Hunting's Patchwork Collection consists of a
chair, a book box, and twelve lamps that fit inside each
other like babushka dolls. The collection was handmade
with waste timber collected from factories in Denmark.
Astonishingly, each piece was made without screws or
bolts; hidden timber dowel connects the parts. Each
piece is slightly different, with various timbers assembled
into playful patchwork patterns of colour and grain.

\01: An imperfect quality characterises the sculpting of the chair legs. Timbers are contrasted, as are fabrics in patchwork sewing.

The book box incorporates built-in stands that – depending on the orientation of the box – can serve as legs, horizontal ledges, or vertical supports against which books of various heights may be leant. The box can be stacked or hung on a wall. The chair takes on a caricature-like quality thanks to the intentionally imperfect carving of its legs and their contrasts of timber colour.

Norwegian-British designer Amy Hunting (London, UK) studied furniture and spatial design at The Danish Design School. She worked for Established & Sons before setting up her own practice in London. Along with developing and making furniture, Amy is a freelance illustrator. She enjoys seeking ways in which she can combine her passion for drawings and illustrations with furniture. Portrait courtesy of Amy Hunting.

www.amyhunting.com

Patchwork Furniture by Amy Hunting

Turn to page 258 to read about Amy Hunting's Patchwork Lamp. Another of her designs, Blockshelf, is featured on page 116.

\02: The multi-directional book box can house books of various sizes. Right: one of Amy's conceptual drawings.

made in peckham

by Hendzel and Hunt

Photographs by Ed Kulakowski

A sense of honesty emanates from the Made in Peckham range of furniture. The seats and tables are constructed with reclaimed and waste timber such as discarded floorboards and pallets. The timber is collected from the streets and wood yards of London's SE15 district, which includes the designers' own neighbourhood of Peckham. A considerable history of use can be read in the timber's flaked paint, nail holes, and scratches.

\01: The Hinckley Table and Kirkwood Chairs, photographed in a wood yard, draw out the beauty of unique scrap materials.

Beyond the obvious honesty expressed in the condition of the timber, there is also a clarity and directness in the construction techniques used to assemble the furniture. Designer-makers Hendzel and Hunt work with traditional cabinetmakers' jointing techniques, using timber dowel to peg together pieces of timber. They avoid metal fixings of any kind.

Hendzel and Hunt (London, UK) was established by Jan Hendzel (left) and Oscar Hunt (right). The studio specialises in the design and manufacture of bespoke cabinets and furniture. Jan is a patternmaking engineer with seven years' experience. He studied product design at Central St Martins College of Art and Design in London. Oscar is a joiner and lighting designer. He studied three-dimensional design for production at the University of Brighton. Portraits by Ed Kulakowski.

www.hendzelandhunt.com

Made in Peckham by Hendzel and Hunt

\02: The base of the Hinckley Table is akin to a heavy-duty sculpture of interlocking timber.

\03: Many layers of flaked paint can be seen on some of the timber surfaces, suggesting the material's history of use.

The Kirkwood Chairs are made with two types of timber waste. The frames are crafted with reclaimed hardwood, and the seats and backrests are made with floorboards from the Victorian era. The assembly of the boards in strips of alternating (existing) finishes gives the chairs a graphic quality. The Gowlett Stools are compositions of wood from discarded pallets found outside the designers' studio. The application of eco-friendly paint brings aesthetic cohesion with the chairs.

The top of the Hinckley Table is an intricate configuration of pallet pieces. Its base is a formation of six interlocking lengths of reclaimed hardwood, fixed in place with two large dowels. The Made in Peckham range is batch-produced in small numbers. Due to the very nature – and limited availability – of reclaimed materials, every piece of furniture is unique.

Made in Peckham by Hendzel and Hunt

\04: The jointing techniques used to construct the Gowlett Stool are clearly evident in its form.

off-cut seat

by Gitta Gschwendtner

Photographs courtesy of Gitta Gschwendtner

The timber offcuts produced by industries such as furniture manufacturing are usually either too small to use or impossible to machine. "Many factories in cold climates burn this waste to generate heat during the winter months," explained London-based designer Gitta Gschwendtner. "But some of the solid timber found in the waste piles is simply too beautiful to end its life in the furnace."

Gitta created the stool with offcuts generated by Benchmark Furniture – a design-led manufacturer established by Terence Conran and Sean Sutcliffe. Benchmark obtains its timbers from sustainable sources.

\01: The Off-Cut Seat shows off the random nature of the timber stack through its simple shape.

With offcuts from a UK-based furniture manufacturer, Gitta created a stool for design collective TEN's exhibition *TEN XYZ*. The show investigated sustainability within design that uses digital manufacturing technologies. The timber offcuts were sawn to a uniform thickness and glued in a random stack formation. A digitally generated minimal stool shape was then milled from the stack by a five-axis CNC machine.

Gitta Gschwendtner (London, UK) was born in Germany, but has lived in the UK since studying at Central Saint Martins College of Art and Design, Kingston University, and the Royal College of Art. In 1998, she established an independent design studio for furniture, interior design, exhibition design, and public art projects. Gitta's clients hail from the cultural, arts, and corporate arenas. Her studio focuses on conceptually rigorous and functional designs. Portrait courtesy of Gitta Gschwendtner.

www.gittagschwendtner.com

Off-Cut Seat by Gitta Gschwendtner

\02: Left: the digital model. Bottom right: the stack was quite loose, with negative spaces enhancing the stool's appearance.

800g library

by Dany Gilles

Photographs by Dany Gilles

How lightweight can a bookshelf be before it collapses under the weight of its contents? Designer Dany Gilles investigated this using a modular design approach and a material whose low mass and structural performance are well known. He devised a modular shelf unit with scrap cardboard that weighs – as its name suggests – just 800 grams.

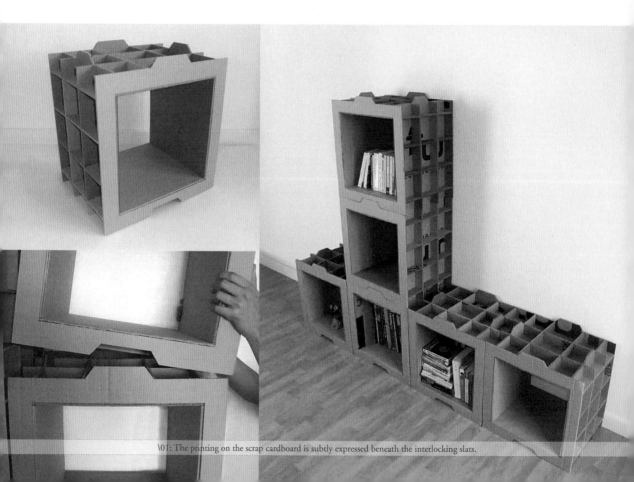

\01: The printing on the scrap cardboard is subtly expressed beneath the interlocking slats.

The 800g Library is a composition of slotted and glued pieces of double-layered corrugated cardboard. Each unit contains twenty-two parts that are digitally cut from reclaimed cardboard. When assembled, they create a rigid structure. The units can be stacked, with interlocking frame elements resisting lateral movement. While the inner surfaces of the cube are lined, the outer surfaces expose the interlocked structure in order to keep weight to a minimum.

Designer and interior designer Dany Gilles (Bourg-lès-Valence, France) studied at ESAM Design (l'Ecole Supérieur des Arts Modernes) in Paris. His professional design activities are split between private projects and those undertaken in association with architect Patrick Nadeau, designer Jean-Baptiste Sibertin-Blanc, and the Hermès brand. Another of Dany's upcycling projects involved the transformation of surplus advertising posters into moulded seats using a paper mâché technique. Portrait by Dany Gilles.

www.danygilles.com

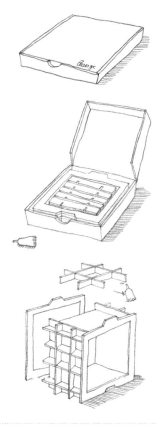

800g Library by Dany Gilles

\02: The shelf unit has been designed for flat packing. Each unit measures 460 (l) x 350 (w) x 460 (h) mm.

life after corkage

by Phase Design
Photographs by Phase Design

The Life After Corkage bar stool and ottoman can be looked upon as receptacles of experiences – of the happiness, sadness, and every other feeling associated with a bottle of wine. Designer Reza Feiz (the founder of Phase Design) had been focusing on cork as a design material for some time. "Each cork has a wonderful scent, appearance, and history. I began to feel silly discarding such a beautiful object with each bottle of wine," he explained.

\01: The ottoman has an 18-in (460-mm) diameter and a height of 15in (380mm). The bar stool stands 31in (790mm) high.

The barstool gives a second life to 1,200 used corks that would otherwise be discarded. The ottoman contains 2,500 reclaimed corks. Vinyl-coated threaded polyester mesh contains the mass of corks. The mesh is loose enough to allow for breathability. It also allows the corks' markings to be read. The barstool incorporates a frame of powder-coated steel tubing (for indoor use or covered outdoor use) or stainless steel tubing (for exposed outdoor use).

Self-taught designer Reza Feiz (Los Angeles, USA) founded Phase Design in 2000. The studio produces furniture, lighting, planters, and tabletop products with a philosophy of "strength in simplicity." Reza favours handcrafting and has all of Phase Design's pieces produced by artisans located in the USA. The studio has a high-profile client list that includes brands such as Gucci, Tom Ford, Yale University, and L'Oreal USA. Portrait by Eric Axene.

www.phasedesignonline.com

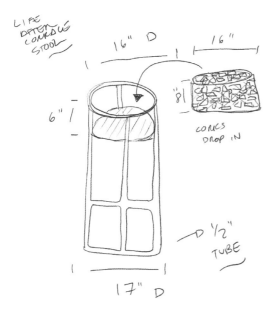

Reza Feiz's interest in designing with used corks was piqued by his visit to a wine cork manufacturing facility in Portugal, where he witnessed the extensive work goes into their manufacture.

Life After Corkage by Phase Design

\02: The cork cushion can be removed from the bar stool frame, in which it fits snugly.

t-shirt chair

by Maria Westerberg

Photographs by Maria Westerberg

The work of designer Maria Westerberg is based on the creation of new uses for found objects and materials. Her T-shirt Chair provides a new life for forty old t-shirts. The garments are woven through a single sheet of bent metal grid. The chair's proportions and the grade of the grid sheeting were specified to suit the average size and bulk of an adult's t-shirt.

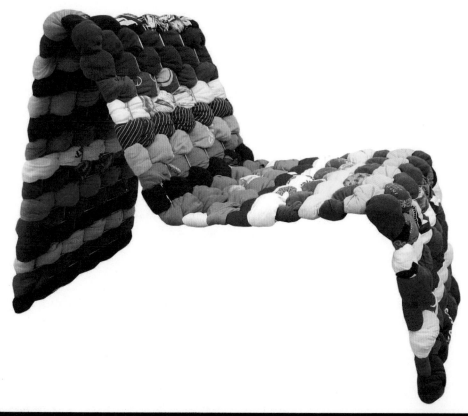

\01: The t-shirts used in the prototype were donated by Maria's friends, colleagues, and family members.

Maria felt that the classic unisex t-shirt can reflect one's personality more than any other piece of clothing as it usually displays a print related to the wearer – for example, a sporting team or musician's logo, or the name of a holiday destination. Her intention was for the chair to preserve the stories attached to the garments. The t-shirts can be rearranged or replaced easily. Green Furniture is producing the chair.

Maria Westerberg (Stockholm, Sweden) is inspired by the idea of generating new possibilities for tired objects that already have a history – giving old things a second chance and adding new stories to their histories. Maria studied interior architecture and furniture at Konstfack, and now runs her own studio where she creates one-off pieces and undertakes commissioned projects. Her work is characterised by playfulness and colour. She formerly studied oil painting and the science of art. Portrait by Stefan Jellheden.

www.mariawesterberg.se

T-shirt Chair by Maria Westerberg

\02: The chair is reminiscent of traditional rag rugs, in which fabric scraps are braided or woven together.

03. lighting

multi-vase lighting

by Atelier Remy & Veenhuizen

Photographs courtesy of Atelier Remy & Veenhuizen

An animated quality emanates from the Multi-vase Lighting, though dynamism is not a characteristic one would usually associate with glassware or light fixtures. These compositions of glass vases, jugs, bowls, and light shades appear to have been thrown into the air and frozen in time. In fact, they are connected with transparent glue and hung from a single point – the handle of a jug or mug.

\01: Light is either contained by or directed towards items of coloured glass.

The compositions seem ad hoc, but each element has been positioned with intent – either to direct a light source or to preserve the functionality of a vessel. As such, Multi-vase can be used to accommodate small everyday items such as keys, change, bus tickets, pencils, and so on. Common and outdated household items are granted a new life and a new function in these interactive lighting installations.

Tejo Remy and René Veenhuizen (Utrecht, The Netherlands) work together as product, interior, and public space designers. Their work explores the possibilities inherent in found goods and materials. They aim to create new meanings by using such objects and materials in alternate ways and contexts, thereby engaging the users of their objects on multiple levels.

www.remyveenhuizen.nl

Multi-vase Lighting by
Atelier Remy & Veenhuizen

relumine

by mischer'traxler

Photographs by mischer'traxler

The phase-out of incandescent light bulbs and the switch to new energy-saving globes inspired Austrian studio mischer'traxler to rethink the shape and nature of lamps. Rather than design an entirely new lamp form, however, the designers opted to reuse and redefine discarded floor and table lamps. Taking various forms, the Relumine lamps each incorporate two disused old lamps connected by a fluorescent tube.

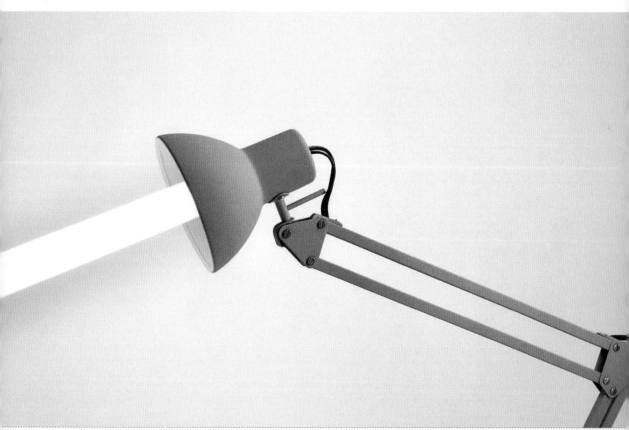

\01: A familiar lamp form takes on a surreal new character thanks to the redefinition of its light source.

The old lamps are disassembled, sanded, re-lacquered, and adapted with new technology before being connected. The introduction of a new type of light source to the old lamps significantly alters their character, and together the two lamps require less energy to function than each one did in its previous life. Relumine uses T5 fluorescent tubes, which are available in several light colours.

Katharina Mischer and Thomas Traxler (Vienna, Austria) graduated from the master's course (conceptual design in context) at the Design Academy Eindhoven. They established mischer'traxler in 2009 to develop products, furniture, and exhibitions with an experimental and conceptual approach. mischer'traxler aims to look differently at people's habits and surroundings, posing new questions and interpreting new answers. This practice often leads to integrated concepts, systems, and visions, instead of single products. Portrait by mischer'traxler.

www.mischertraxler.com

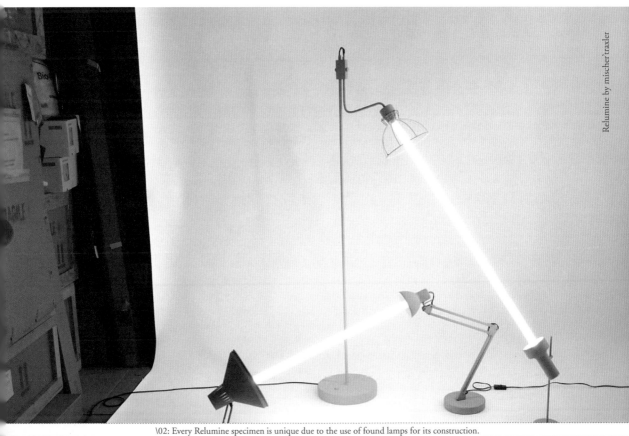

Relumine by mischer'traxler

\02: Every Relumine specimen is unique due to the use of found lamps for its construction.

\03: Depending on the height and scale of the original lamps, Relumine could be used as either ambient or task lighting.

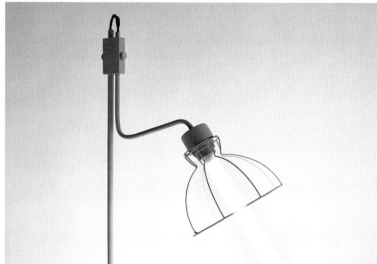

Relumine by mischer'traxler

Relumine was originally designed for an exhibition titled *Bulb Fiction*, which was held at Gallery Klaus Engelhorn during Vienna Design Week in 2010.

\04: Relumine allows for new and varied spatial relationships between the user and the light source.

tools table lamp

by Fabien Dumas

Photographs courtesy of Fabien Dumas

During Milan Design Week in 2011, the Ventura Lambrate design district featured an exhibition that explored the experimental 'making' aspect of the design process. Titled *Poetry Happens*, the exhibition displayed archetypal prototyped objects and installations with a narrative design quality. The exhibition was curated by designers Fabien Dumas, Werner Aisslinger, and Tim Brauns.

\01: Vertical support is provided by a timber member at the base of the lamp.

Fabien's own contribution to the show was an exploration of the poetry of material, collage, and sustainability. Tools Table Lamp was imagined as a hybrid object that is neither a lamp nor a ruler, but is both an archetype and an everyday item. Made with parts form an old lamp and extendible wooden rulers, Tools turns the common into the uncommon and creates something new with something known.

Product designer Fabien Dumas (Berlin, Germany) studied industrial design at the Berlin University of the Arts. During his studies he worked as a freelance designer on several projects with department stores such as KaDeWe and Galeries Lafayette. After graduating, he worked as a freelance designer for Arne Quinze at Quinze & Milan in Kortrijk, Belgium. Recently, Fabien has designed objects for brands such as Ingo Maurer, Dark, and Marset. Portrait courtesy of Fabien Dumas.

www.toomanydesigners.net

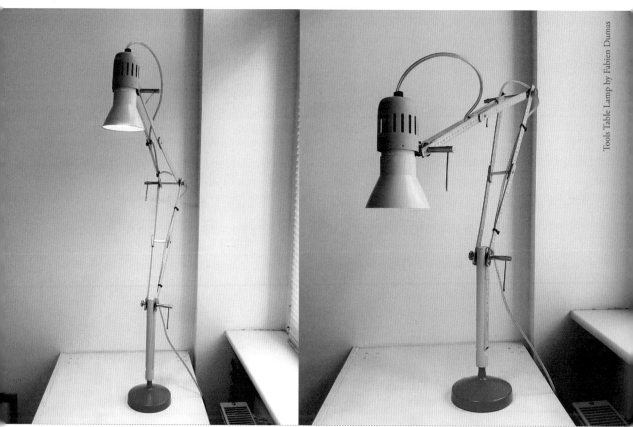

Tools Table Lamp by Fabien Dumas

\02: The adjustable nature of the wooden rulers is mirrored in their new role as the arm of the table lamp.

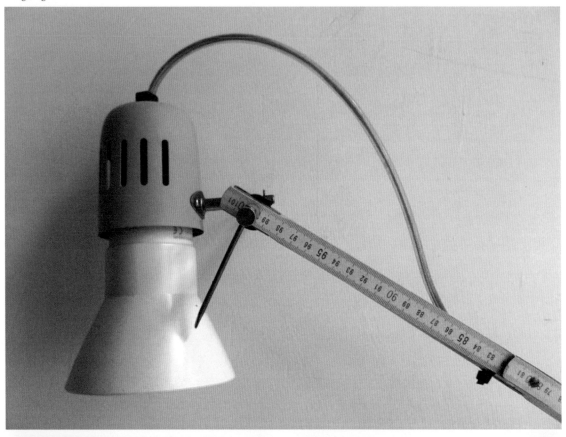

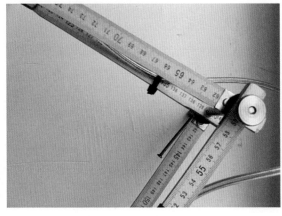

\03: Winding levers indicate the moving joints. The electrical cord is attached to the rulers with cable ties.

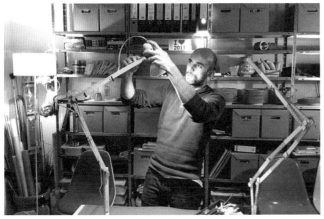

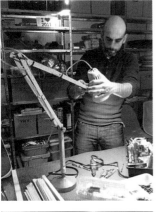

Tools Table Lamp by Fabien Dumas

\04: Tools also explores the poetry of prototyping – the story and evolution of the creative process.

SMP lights

by Sergio Mendoza Studio

Photographs by Sergio Mendoza

Since 2005, Sergio Mendoza has been part of a small team responsible for organising the Vitra Summer Workshops at Domaine de Boisbuchet – a rural property in the south-west of France. The workshops are akin to a creative camp; the participants live at the property and explore projects under the guidance of renowned designers, architects, and artists. One of Sergio's projects investigated the use of found materials to create lamps.

\01: The rapid construction method involved techniques such as gluing and stapling the rough-edged pieces of crate.

Fruit and vegetables are delivered to the property daily in wooden crates, which cannot be reused and are burnt every night. Sergio devised the SMP Lights by applying simple construction techniques to pieces of the crates. He was able to build a light in less than one hour. Given that the material is not one normally used in the context of domestic interiors, Sergio gave the lights an archetypal shape that would be familiar and comforting.

Sergio Mendoza (Valencia, Spain) is a product designer, but his creative pursuits also include graphic design, photography, and interior design. He studied industrial design and post-graduate product design at UCH–CEU (University Cardenal Herrera) in Valencia, and now combines freelance work with the art direction of the Maratón Fotográfico de Valencia. Along with his work at the Vitra Summer Workshops, he is also a photographer for fashionalistas.com and directs someoneimet.com. Portrait courtesy of Sergio Mendoza.

www.sergio-mendoza.com

SMP Lights by Sergio Mendoza Studio

\02: A small white porcelain vase was also used as a lampshade. All components of the lights are visible; nothing is concealed.

invisible chandelier

by Castor

Photographs copyright Derek Shapton

Like a cumulus cloud, the Invisible Chandelier is
a hovering accumulated form. One can imagine
this composition of burnt-out light bulbs growing
organically as each bulb expires and is replaced – just as
a cloud accumulates water droplets. Of course, its form
is static. However, the Invisible Chandelier provides an
engaging visual record of the various mediums through
which light is delivered.

\01: The seemingly haphazard composition of used light bulbs has a standard size of 1.5ft (0.45m) wide, 1ft (0.3m) deep, and 5ft (1.5m) or 3ft (0.9m) long.

It can be viewed as a specimen that encourages contemplation of the choices we make as consumers of electrical energy. The bulbs – which range in variety from incandescent, to energy-saving, halogen, floodlight, and more – are sourced mainly from re-lamping companies. They are wired to a powder-coated metal frame and the mass is lit from within by three halogen bulbs. Two standard sizes are produced, but the chandelier can also be customised.

Castor (Toronto, Canada) is Brian Richer and Kei Ng. The studio creates uncommon objects – often by recontextualising used materials – and also undertakes spatial and graphic design. Recently, Castor has worked on projects with interior designers and architects, creating custom light installations and furniture. Brian trained as an architectural stone carver and studied English literature and philosophy at York University. Kei studied architecture at the University of Winnipeg prior to many years art directing films and running a restaurant. Portrait by Jessica Eaton.

www.castordesign.ca

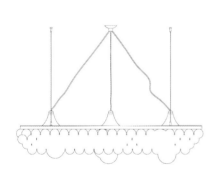

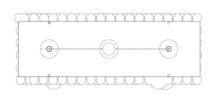

Invisible Chandelier by Castor

hanger lamps

by Luís Teixeira / 1961ecodesign

Photographs by Fabrice Ziegler

Portuguese designer Luís Teixeira is deeply concerned about environmental issues and today's prevalent patterns of easy consumption. His feelings of unease have prompted him to seek alternatives to industrial mass production for his own products. The use of reclaimed materials has become a priority, as has an approach of handcrafting. Luís aims to change people's mentality about waste material by showing possibilities for its reuse.

\01: The Noova lamp weighs around 3.2kg and has a diameter of 620mm. The plastic takes on a glass-like appearance when lit.

But there is more to his social agenda. Some of his objects are handcrafted by people in long-term unemployment as well as those in prison. "This provides a way to prepare people for the labour market, giving them a source of income and enhancing their self-esteem," Luís explains. He also sees it as an opportunity to connect people with design thinking. His Hanger Lamp titled Noova is produced in a women's prison in Tires, Portugal.

After graduating from studies in the history of art, Luís Teixeira (Lisbon, Portugal) found his attention turning to the design of products. He established 1961ecodesign as a vehicle for the creation of lighting, furniture, and other objects with reclaimed materials. Among his other products are a light shade and necklaces made with juice package caps, and table lamps made with old vinyl records or disposable plastic dishes. Portrait by Fabrice Ziegler.

www.facebook.com/luis.teixeira.1961ecodesign

Hanger Lamps by
Luís Teixeira / 1961ecodesign

\02 The hangers' central rail hooks are hidden within the Noova lamp. The undersides of the hangers are exposed.

The lamps are made with disposable plastic hangers that would otherwise be discarded after the sale of women's underwear. Each lamp incorporates a minimum of seventy-five per cent reused materials. The plastic hangers are hooked onto metal frames (akin to typical lampshade frames) that also support the electric components.

The disc-like Noova lamp was made with 210 hangers, and consists of two cone-shaped constructions joined at their widest point. Joanna V incorporates 220 hangers. Its shape was developed from the Noova base. Eggo contains 400 hangers, and its shape was developed as a globe.

\03: The Eggo lamp (left) is the largest and heaviest lamp in the range, weighing 6.9kg. Joanna V (right) weighs 3.75kg.

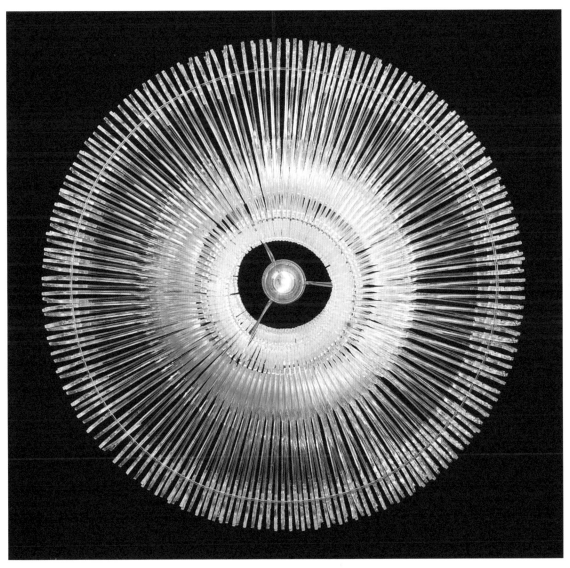

Hanger Lamps by
Luís Teixeira / 1961ecodesign

\04: Viewed from beneath, the Noova lamp reveals how the hangers are fanned outwards to create the lamp shape.

light reading

by Lula Dot

Photographs by Lucy Norman

Many thousands of used paperback books are donated to charities every year. So many, says British designer Lucy Norman of Lula Dot, that most go unsold. Often, she says, the charities need to pay for the excess books to be transported to landfill. Furthermore, Lucy has been unable to find any established infrastructure for the recycling of the paper from paperback books because the paper is of a low grade and the glue on the spine must be removed.

\01: Fragments of the books' contents can be seen at the cut (rounded) and folded (straight) edges of the pages.

She designed the Light Reading chandelier as part of a larger range of objects made with disused books. A circular hole is cut through each of the six paperback books and every page is folded in half before the book is fanned out and the covers are joined. A framework of steel rods holds the books in place around a central globe. Small metal plates support the books at the base of each vertical rod.

Lucy Norman (London, UK) established Lula Dot in 2009 with the aim of transforming London's waste into products ranging from furniture to jewellery. She also works as a freelance designer. Her freelance projects have ranged from retail display systems, to product design, to set design for a theatre. Lucy studied product design at the University of Brighton. She is pictured here with another of Lula Dot's products – a lamp made with the necks and caps of PET bottles. Portrait by Lucy Norman.

www.luladot.com

Light Reading by Lula Dot

Lula Dot also offers the Paperback Partition – a room divider filled with regularly sized books that plays on the idea of a bookshelf.

\02: The lamp is suspended on three wires that are hung from the ceiling.

anglepoise lamp and factory slide

by Henry Wilson

Photographs by Rene van der Hulst and Nichon Glerum

Why design new things for an oversaturated world when so many good products already exist? Designer Henry Wilson grappled with this question, providing an answer with Things Revisited – a collection of objects that resulted from his 'interference' with classic designs. With the intention of transforming the old into something new and desirable, he made discreet updates that slightly altered the appearance and function of the objects.

\01: The Anglepoise Lamp is pictured here with other objects from the Things Revisited collection.

Subtlety and honesty were key elements in Henry's design approach. He altered only the light source and shade of the Anglepoise Lamp, for example, leaving the refined engineered form of the industrial lamp base untouched. The shade, remade in glass, was fitted with a near-invisible low-energy LED. The enamel shade of the Factory Slide lamp was split and fitted with a translucent bone china sleeve. As such, the lamp can offer 360-degree light as well as focused downcast light.

Henry Wilson (Sydney, Australia) earned his master's degree at the Design Academy Eindhoven. His studies investigated the desire for the 'new' that seems built into the psyche of today's consumers. With his Things Revisited collection, he proposed a way to satisfy this desire and pay tribute to things that last. Henry's work seeks a balance between conceptual thinking and the nature of the everyday. His current projects range from fashion to furniture, products, and interiors. Portrait by Axel Arnott.

www.henry-wilson.com

Anglepoise Lamp and Factory Slide by Henry Wilson

\02: The Factory Slide's new translucent sleeve makes its light dimmer and more appropriate for domestic use.

other people's rubbish, collection 1

by Heath Nash

Photographs courtesy of Heath Nash

When exploring ways he might convey a distinctly South African identity in his products, designer Heath Nash contemplated and experimented with galvanised steel wire – a typical local craft material. A chance meeting with a wire artist who was also working with used plastic bottles provided a new inspiration. The practice of reuse as a typically South African mode of production resonated strongly with Heath.

\01: The multicoloured Flowerdrum is made with hand-cut and hand-creased flower and butterfly shapes. Photo by Dave Southwood.

After some experimentation, he devised a way to produce lights with a combination of wire and post-consumer plastic bottles. Other People's Rubbish was born with the Leafball – a composition of hand-creased plastic 'leaves' (cut from used bottles) attached to a handmade wire structure with cable ties. Most of the subsequent lights were designed with the same construction system.

Heath Nash (Cape Town, South Africa) established the Heath Nash company in 2005, having previously completed fine arts studies at the University of Cape Town (majoring in sculpture). The company produces Heath's own product range, as well as commissioned pieces. The studio-based team is paralleled by an off-site team of local plastic selectors, cutters, creasers, and wire workers. When exhibiting internationally, Heath runs workshops for adults and children, demonstrating the potential of their plastic waste. Portrait courtesy of Heath Nash.

www.heathnash.com

Other People's Rubbish, Collection 1 by Heath Nash

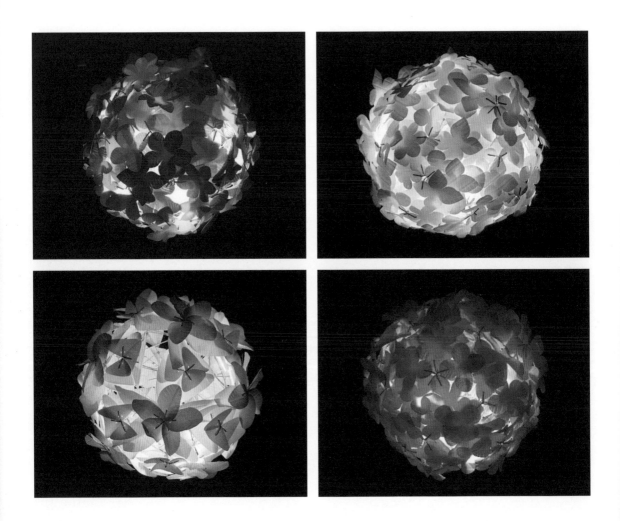

\03: Clockwise from top left – a small multicoloured Flowerball; a white Flowerball; a pink Flowerball; and the original Leafball in white.

Other People's Rubbish, Collection 1
by Heath Nash

\04: A lamp was also developed with a base of plastic bottles and a bucket shade. Photo by Dave Southwood.

other people's rubbish, collection 2

by Heath Nash

Photographs courtesy of Heath Nash

Other People's Rubbish was developed by Heath Nash to create products with a distinct South African identity, but also as a way to generate employment opportunities. He explained, "I realised that by using the right knowledge and materials – wire and plastic – combined with typically South African skills and contemporary design, a new aesthetic could be created which really spoke to the current South African situation." He also aimed to promote the idea of reuse.

\01: The Bottleformball is composed with sections of bottles on a handmade wire structure. Photo by Dave Southwood.

Whereas the ball and drum lamps in the first collection of Other People's Rubbish are made with only the flat sections of plastic bottles, the second collection makes use of the 'hidden shapes' within the bottles – the handles, bases, openings, and so on. Wire components as well as waxed thread are used to bind together these more complex forms, which are cut by hand from cleaned reclaimed bottles of various shapes.

Heath Nash (Cape Town, South Africa) established the Heath Nash company in 2005, having previously completed fine arts studies at the University of Cape Town (majoring in sculpture). The company produces Heath's own product range, as well as commissioned pieces. The studio-based team is paralleled by an off-site team of local plastic selectors, cutters, creasers, and wire workers. When exhibiting internationally, Heath runs workshops for adults and children, demonstrating the potential of their plastic waste. Portrait courtesy of Heath Nash.

www.heathnash.com

Other People's Rubbish, Collection 2 by Heath Nash

\02: Yoghurt bottles, fabric softener bottle handles, and milk bottle handles compose the Bottleball, Pod, and Milkhandleform Ball (clockwise from top left).

cablelamps

by Vij5

Photographs by Merel van Beukering

For a variety of reasons, Dutch designers Vij5 enjoy using existing objects in their products or allowing them to influence their designs. In some instances, found objects offer functional benefits. In others, they offer a way to encourage people to think differently about the products or elements we are surrounded with on a daily basis. Such was the case for the CableLamps.

\01: By combining it with old-fashioned lamps, the designers wished to encourage feelings of sentimentality for electric cable.

This collection of table and ceiling lamps uses power cable as a decorative element. "Everything is becoming wireless these days," explain the designers. "For that reason we wished to pay tribute to electric cables, which are quickly disappearing from our lives." The black cable is wound onto the lampshade frames of a range of second-hand lamps. Every lamp is different, and the application of the cable is customised to each lampshade shape. Limited editions of the lamps are produced.

Vij5 (Eindhoven, the Netherlands) was founded by designers and entrepreneurs Arjan van Raadshooven and Anieke Branderhorst. The brand offers a collection of interior products designed by Arjan and Anieke, but the pair also collaborates with other young designers. Vij5 is currently collaborating with Mieke Meijer, who devised a way to upcycle old newspapers into a new material called NewspaperWood. The team recently invited young Dutch designers to experiment with NewspaperWood for the development of a product collection. Portrait by Patricia Rehe.

www.vij5.com

CableLamps by Vij5

\02: The lampshade frames are wrapped with a single continuous length of cable.

nine inch nails

by Giovanni Delvecchio and Andrea Magnani
for Resign

Photographs by Marco Piffari

Nine Inch Nails is a series of lamps that combines electrical components with parts from typical office chairs. Specifically, the spine, legs, and wheels of discarded chairs are salvaged. The result is light source that can be rolled across the floor and tucked under tables. An abstract animal-like quality prevails thanks to the lamps' legged forms and their ability to be moved around a space – a ready accompaniment to human endeavours.

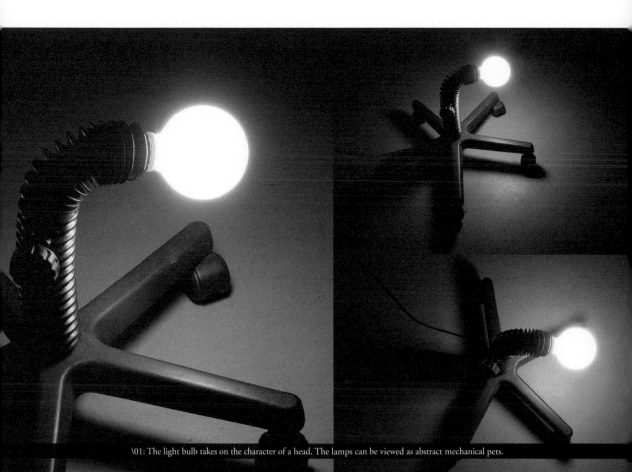

\01: The light bulb takes on the character of a head. The lamps can be viewed as abstract mechanical pets.

Resign (Faenza, Italy) is a "meta-project" consisting of a physical atelier space and a network of relationships. At its core is the promotion of a sustainable approach to design – from both an environmental and social perspective. Objects are regarded not from an aesthetic point of view, but with consideration of their ability to create human relationships and express identity. The Resign project facilitates design activities, research, education and training, and professional advice.

Giovanni Delvecchio and Andrea Magnani (Faenza, Italy) founded Resign with Elisabetta Amatori in 2007. Andrea describes himself as a "reality curator" and Giovanni views himself as a "door-to-door designer." The pair studied together at the Istituto Superiore per le Industrie Artistiche (ISIA) in Faenza. They seek to change people's perspectives of reality. Portrait courtesy of Resign.

www.resign.it

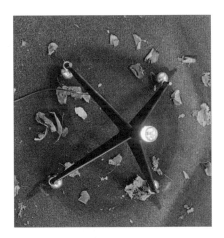

Nine Inch Nails by Giovanni Delvecchio and Andrea Magnani for Resign

Turn to page 018 to see Resign's Abitudini clothes hangers, which are made with the backs of old chairs.

\02: Different chair styles lead to varied characters in the lamps.

wildfor lamp

by Fordesignfor

Photographs courtesy of Serena Riccardi

The Wildfor Lamp gives the impression that it might suddenly break its static pose and move. Its three legs – skeletal and bent at various angles – resemble the segmented limbs of an insect. The bulb seems to stare like an eye. The lamp's shade, however, was modelled on the carnivorous Venus Flytrap plant, whose hair-lined leaves snap shut to trap insects that traverse them.

\01: The electrical cable is neatly hidden with the lamp's gently curved stem.

The lamp is made entirely from reclaimed materials. The stem and legs are made with metal tubing sourced from old clothes racks. Two centrally aligned fan grills form the leaves of the shade. The electrical system incorporates a 15-watt fluorescent energy-saving bulb with a life span of 8,000 hours. The red and green paint is water-based and has low VOC emission levels.

Industrial designer Luca Gnizio (Milan, Italy) established Fordesignfor in 2007 with the aim of transforming recovered materials into furniture. He seeks ways to turn objects and materials discarded by factories and industry in general into desirable and functional designs that will enrich daily life. Prior to establishing his own brand, Luca created prototypes for large companies, and also worked in the fields of interior and packaging design. Portrait courtesy of Serena Riccardi.

www.fordesignfor.com

Wildfor Lamp by Fordesignfor

\02: Mimicking the colours of the Venus Flytrap plant, the lampshade's outer shell is painted green on its outer surface.

\03: Reclaimed tubular steel elbows function as small stabilising feet.

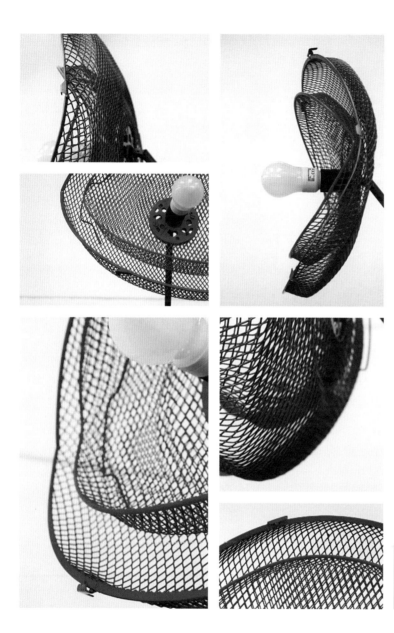

Read about Luca Gnizio's Bookfor Armchair (a composition of reclaimed reinforcing bars and textiles) on page 170.

Wildfor Lamp by Fordesignfor

\04: The two fan grills are bent to hint at the shape of the Venus Flytrap's leaf blades – and reinforce the lamp's 'wild' character.

tableware lamps

by Oddbirds

Photographs by Anders Jungermark

The members of Swedish design collective Oddbirds view flea markets as treasure chests – destinations for cups, teapots, and bowls that people's grandparents probably hoarded and cherished for decades. The designers select what they consider to be the most beautiful pieces of porcelain and stoneware. They drill through them, stack them, and install electrical components to create unique lamp bases.

\01: Each style of lamp composition is named. Gunnar (left) and Silvia (right) are made with stoneware from the 1960s and '70s.

The change of context in which the tableware is used encourages a 'rediscovery' of each cup, saucer, bowl, vase, plate, or teapot – a fresh contemplation of each form, despite the familiarity that many people will find in them. The design harks back to the domestic craft tradition of turning empty glass bottles into lamp bases. Every lamp is unique and numbered.

Oddbirds (Tranemo, Sweden) refers to itself as a 'creative nest' where designers make things their own way. The collective takes an approach of cross-fertilisation, mixing colours, shapes, and functions at will. The result could be a lamp, a notebook, a necklace, or a cushion. Old, reclaimed, and new materials are adopted and different expressions are explored in a free-spirited and joyful creative process. Portrait by Anders Jungermark.

www.oddbirds.nu

Tableware Lamps by Oddbirds

\02: The Siv style is made with porcelain of various ages and designs. An upturned bowl forms the base of each piece.

luminária lumi 01

by Mônica Rodrigues Fernandes / Vértices Casa

Photographs by Mozart Fernandes

While observing the public works construction sites around her home in São Paulo, Brazilian designer Mônica Rodrigues Fernandes noticed a variety of temporary timber structures. These makeshift fabrications were developed by the builders to facilitate their daily activities on site – accommodating lighting systems, for example. They were made with the scraps of timber on hand, and assembled in a direct, fuss-free manner.

\01: The directness of the design approach is contrasted with the fine finish applied to the lamp.

Inspired by the simple elegance of these structures, Mônica developed a lamp with waste timber she collected from the construction sites – pieces of plywood, battens, and an old door. She assembled them with the same sense of immediacy, deliberately contrasting the timbers and leaving screws visible. She finished the timber with a clear sealant and attached a spherical bulb with a porcelain socket. In addition to the lamps, mirror frames and hangers were designed.

Prior to establishing design studio and store Vértices Casa with her partner Mozart Fernandes, Mônica Rodrigues Fernandes (São Paulo, Brazil) worked in the film industry doing production as well as acting. Vértices Casa creates scenography, props, and mobile spaces – often with reclaimed wood found in dumpsters. The store also sells the work of a number of Brazilian creatives. Mônica practices photography as a hobby, capturing urban scenes in São Paulo. Portrait by Mozart Fernandes.

www.verticescasa.com.br

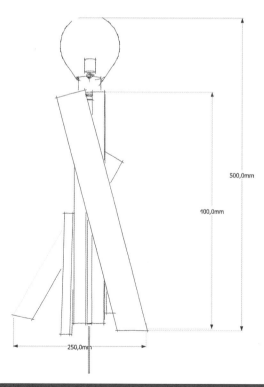

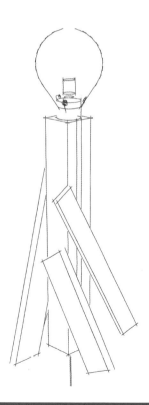

Luminária Lumi 01 by
Mônica Rodrigues Fernandes / Vértices Casa

scrap lights

by Graypants

Photographs courtesy of Graypants

The first Scrap Light was just that – a pendant light made for a friend from cardboard box scraps on the floor of the designers' apartment. The alluring patterns of light and shadow it cast begged further exploration, and American design studio Graypants embarked on the development of a range of Scrap Lights. They retained the handcrafted approach and worked from their shared apartment-cum-studio space.

\01: The designers' intention was to instil a new spirit into lifeless salvaged cardboard, and to create a lively shadow play.

Scrap Lights consist of rings cut from sheets of reclaimed corrugated cardboard, which are stacked and glued into various pendant shapes. As the corrugations are cut at an ever-changing angle, each ring shows a changing edge profile. When Scrap Lights are switched on, wavy patterns of light and shadow appear on nearby surfaces. The cardboard is treated with a non-toxic, low-to-zero VOC, class-A fire retardant.

Jonathan Junker and Seth Grizzle (Seattle, USA) met during their university studies, and launched Graypants as an outlet from their day jobs as young architects. It was a vehicle for making things with their hands. When recession and job loss hit home, the pair found the time to focus on the development of their own studio. The growth of the studio has seen Graypants' work extend from lighting to furniture, architecture, and graphics. Portraits courtesy of Graypants.

www.graypants.com

Scrap Lights by Graypants

\02: Two types of cord are made available – a hardwired cord set with a ceiling canopy kit, and a plug/switch swag set.

Scrap Lights by Graypants

Scrap Lights are produced in bell, disc, hive, bean, olive, drum, squared, twisted, and spherical shapes. They are made with boxes discarded by businesses in Seattle.

\04: Stacks of cardboard rings (and offcuts) prior to final assembly.

patchwork lamp

by Amy Hunting

Photographs courtesy of Amy Hunting

The Patchwork Lamp is part of Amy Hunting's larger Patchwork Collection, which also contains a chair and a book box. The collection was handmade with waste timber collected from factories in Denmark. Each piece is slightly different, with various timbers assembled into playful patchwork patterns of colour and grain. The Patchwork Lamp is a pendant lampshade that can be hung over a bare bulb with no need for fitting.

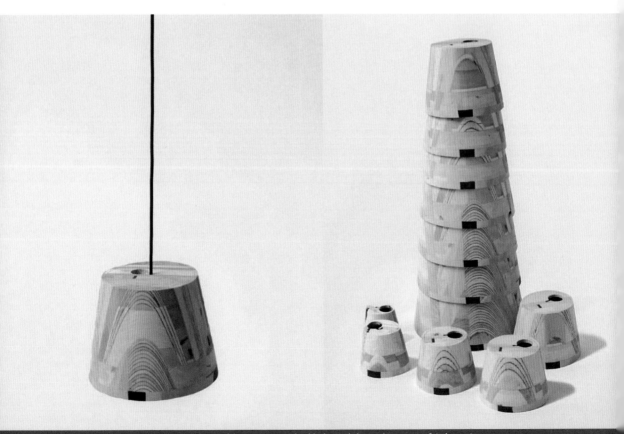

\01: The angular cutting of the composite timber block revealed a graphic pattern of timber grains.

The Patchwork Lamp was produced in twelve sizes that can be stacked inside each other like babushka dolls. Each lampshade was cut from the same block of wood – a composite of small offcuts. One by one, the lampshades were cut from the block at an angle by a bandsaw. At the end of the process, all that remained of the original block was a small piece of wood.

Norwegian-British designer Amy Hunting (London, UK) studied furniture and spatial design at The Danish Design School. She worked for Established & Sons before setting up her own practice in London. Along with developing and making furniture, Amy is a freelance illustrator. She enjoys seeking ways in which she can combine her passion for drawings and illustrations with furniture. Portrait courtesy of Amy Hunting.

www.amyhunting.com

Patchwork Lamp by Amy Hunting

Turn to page 198 to read about Amy Hunting's Patchwork Furniture. Another of her designs, Blockshelf, is featured on page 116.

\02: Cut-outs on the top of each lampshade allow the bulb housing to be fitted within and the electrical cable to be positioned centrally.

glo

by Draigo Design

Photographs by Draigo Design

Glo is an ambient light that transforms standard forty-millimetre plastic bottle caps into a glowing ring-shaped conduit. The components of Glo – 200 bottle caps and a flexible LED tube containing 240 globes – are contained by a lightweight, rigid wireframe structure with a one-metre diameter. Holes are punched in the bottle caps and the LED tube is threaded through them.

\01: Glo's intense and colourful light – along with its durability – encourages playfulness.

The light brings a glow to the bottle caps, but it also spills out through the gaps between them. When Glo is hung against a wall, the visual effect of the escaped light is dramatic. Glo can be easily handled as there is very little heat generated by the highly efficient LEDs, which use less than twenty watts. It is also water resistant. The character of Glo can be varied through the use of different combinations of bottle cap colours.

Adrian Draigo (London, UK) has always been interested in retrieving and collecting things that other people discard. His early one-off designs were mostly made with found objects. Later, he became interested in waste streams – the things people throw out regularly. Designing with waste streams allows objects to be produced in multiples. Adrian's background is in visual arts, photography, film, graphics, and animation. Portrait by Draigo Design.

www.draigo.com

Glo by Draigo Design

\02: Cool to the touch, Glo can be easily handled. This brings flexibility to its use.

\03: The lighting effects change according to how Glo is used and displayed. Shafts of spilled light dramatise a wall.

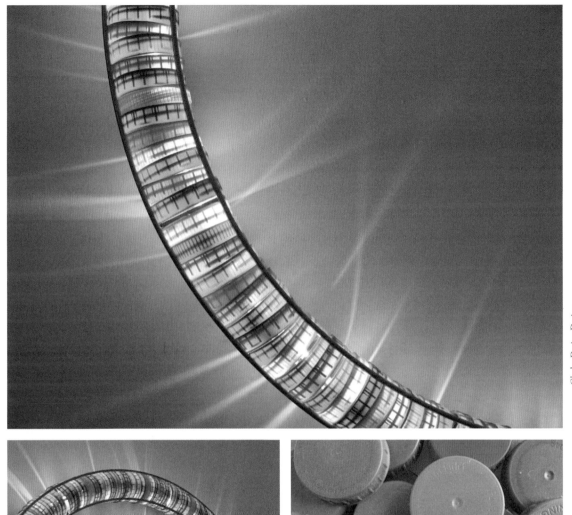

Glo by Draigo Design

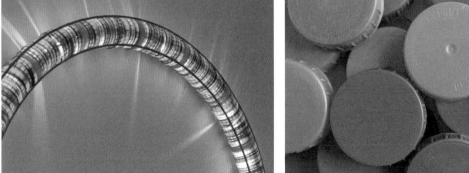

\04: The way the bottle caps settle in the wire structure is random. So too, therefore, are the positions of the gaps through which light escapes.

exploded chandeliers

by Studio Ward van Gemert

Photographs by Adriaan van der Ploeg

Studio Ward van Gemert seeks new expressions for overlooked and discarded items. Ward's intention is to transform existing objects (such as chandeliers and tables) into surprising new designs. While preserving a sense of the past, the revised objects grab attention with their simultaneous familiarity and newness. Explains Ward, "With my interventions, one image can be made to generate an endless number of other images."

\01: The separation of the elements encourages the contemplation of the parts as well as the whole.

To create the Exploded Chandeliers, Ward cuts disused second-hand chandeliers into separate parts using a saw. He reassembles them by threading electrical wire through each component. Some distance is left between the parts, however, with the pieces held in place by metal sleeves on the wire. While it delivers electricity to the globes, the wire also performs a structural role by holding all the parts together. Lengths of aluminium rod are used to separate frame components.

Ward van Gemert (Rotterdam, the Netherlands) established his own studio after graduating from studies in product design at the St Joost Academy of Art and Design in Breda. In his Rotterdam workshop he develops new designs using existing objects, and produces work to order. In collaboration with Adriaan van der Ploeg and Jordan Artisan, Ward has established a second design brand – Nightshop – for the design and production of lamps. Portrait by Adriaan van der Ploeg.

www.wardvangemert.nl

Exploded Chandeliers by Studio Ward van Gemert

\02: The twelve-bulb chandelier (left) reaches 0.95m in width. The twenty-four-bulb version (right) has a width of 1.25m.

The Exploded Chandeliers are made to order. To date, six-bulb, twelve-bulb, and twenty-four-bulb versions have been created, the largest stretching to a diameter of 1.3 metres. Despite the ornamental styles of the original second-hand chandeliers, a modern spirit emerges; the chandeliers can be read as scientific diagrams of their former selves.

The idea of 'exploded' objects first came to Ward during his studies. He developed a series of non-functional exploded chairs for his graduation project. The chairs were cut into pieces and hung from the ceiling with wire. The pieces were positioned in such a way that the existing chairs were transformed into three completely different chairs.

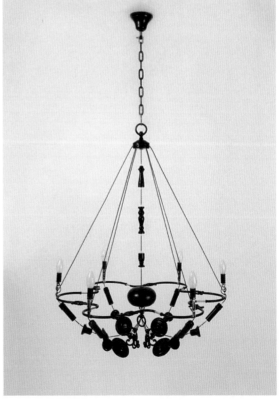

\03: The chandeliers hang from and are powered by the electrical wire.

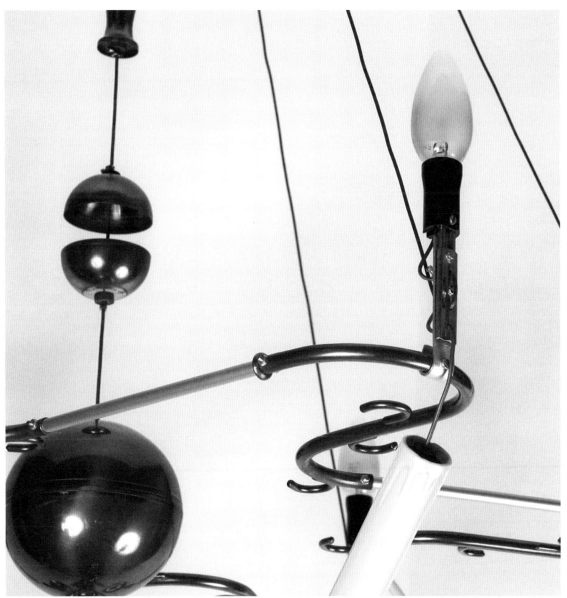

Exploded Chandeliers by
Studio Ward van Gemert

\04: A detail of the six-bulb brass chandelier reveals the use of lightweight aluminium rods as separating elements.

pallet lights

by Studiomama

Photographs courtesy of Studiomama

The Pallet Floor Light and the Pallet X-lamp are part of a wider project by Studiomama that transforms discarded pallets and democratises access to designed goods. The Pallet Project began in 2006 when Nina Tolstrup (founder of Studiomama) designed chairs, a stool, and a floor lamp with pallet wood for an exhibition by London's TEN design collective. Nina's project presented simple, functional furniture and lighting with instructions for its assembly by the consumer.

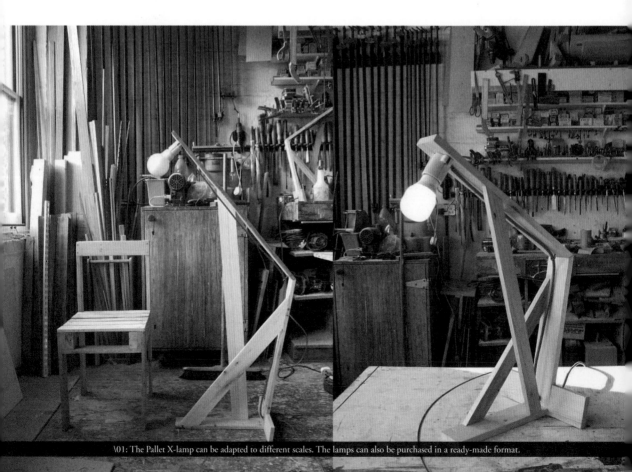

\01: The Pallet X-lamp can be adapted to different scales. The lamps can also be purchased in a ready-made format.

Nina's provision of easy instructions allowed for self-sufficiency along with sustainable consumption. The Pallet Lights shown here follow the same logic. The assembly instructions can be purchased from Studiomama for £10. The floor light is made with one pallet, fifteen screws, a bolt, some reused cable, and a light fitting. Its arm can be swung to vertical and horizontal positions. The X-shaped lamp can be made as a small table lamp or as a larger floor lamp.

Nina Tolstrup (London, UK) trained as a designer at Les Ateliers-Paris Design Institute (ENSCI – École Nationale Supérieure de Création Industrielle). She also studied marketing at the Copenhagen Business School. Through Studiomama, Nina designs, manufactures, and sells her own range of furniture, lights, and other objects. She also designs products for companies, and has undertaken architectural design projects. Cabinets, plant holders, a clock, and a chandelier are also part of Nina's range of pallet-wood objects. Portrait courtesy of Studiomama.

www.studiomama.com

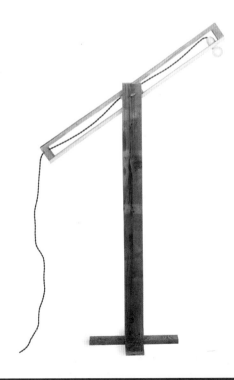

Pallet Lights by Studiomama

\02: The Pallet Floor Light reaches 1.64m in height with its arm in a vertical position, and 1.18m when it is horizontal.

little crush lamp

by Studiomold

Photographs by Studiomold

The Little Crush Lamp combines a no-fuss, lightweight fabric lampshade with an unexpected base – a crushed PET carbonated drink bottle. The bottles are crushed by hand, resulting in a unique sculptural form for every lamp. A black rubber coating provides a sleek finish while concealing the electrical components with the bottles. The coating also allows bottles of various colours to be upcycled with no compromise to the aesthetic direction.

\01: The metal base is raised on short supports. The electrical cord neatly exits the bottle at its base and extends out beneath the plate.

The slight tilt taken on by the lampshade is due to the orientation of the bottle mouth after crushing. A round metal base provides weight and stability. The lamp celebrates imperfection and encourages a reassessment of traditional notions about the aesthetics of form. This buckled light illustrates that various considerations should influence the design process – not merely the idea of a perfected final object.

Studiomold (St Neots, UK) was created by Brendan Young and Vanessa Battaglia, who have been designing furniture and lighting together since 2003. Though they have expanded their portfolio to art direction, interior design, graphics, and communications design, the duo strives to remain faithful to their ideals about sustainable design. They recently founded a new company, Mineheart, for the production of "loveable design." Portrait by Studiomold.

www.studiomold.co.uk

Petcore (a trade association for PET container recycling in Europe, www.petcore.org) reports on its website that 48.4% of all PET bottles on the market in Europe in 2009 were collected for recycling. The bottles are typically shredded into PET flakes that are used to manufacture products such as fibre, strapping, or more PET bottles.

Little Crush Lamp by Studiomold

cuisine d'objets

by 5.5 designers

Photographs courtesy of 5.5 designers

Take a jug, a pot, a bowl, or a vase. Find a branch, the handle from an old broom or mop, a broken chair leg, or something similar. Dig out a clamp spotlight and a permanent marker. Now you're ready to cook. Mix some cement and water in your vessel. Stir the mixture with the stem. Let the cement set, then clamp on your spotlight and sign with "5.5" and your name. Enjoy your home-cooked lamp!

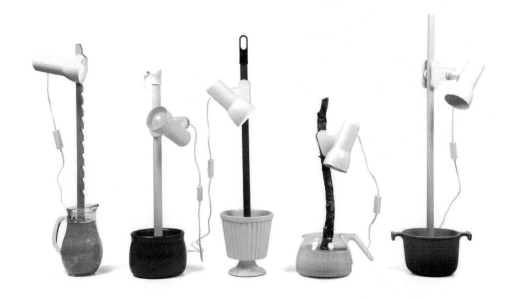

\01: The height and direction of the spotlight can be adjusted simply by re-clamping it as required.

Cuisine d'Objets (which translates from French as "Kitchen Objects") presents a range of 'recipes' for furniture and lighting that can be homemade. A coat rack, a stool, and a magazine holder are also on the menu, as described in the Furniture chapter of this book. The concept allows people to make objects with whatever disused objects are at hand, and adjust the recipes to suit their tastes – as though they were cooking food.

Vincent Baranger, Jean-Sébastien Blanc, Anthony Lebossé, and Claire Renard (Paris, France) established 5.5 designers in 2003. The group works with a commitment to conceptual rigour, and constantly questions their role and status as designers. Their quest for honest and accessible consumption alternatives lends a touch of humour to their work. They have designed products and environments for clients such as Centre Pompidou, Urban Outfitters, and Baccarat. Portrait courtesy of 5.5 designers.

www.cinqcinqdesigners.com

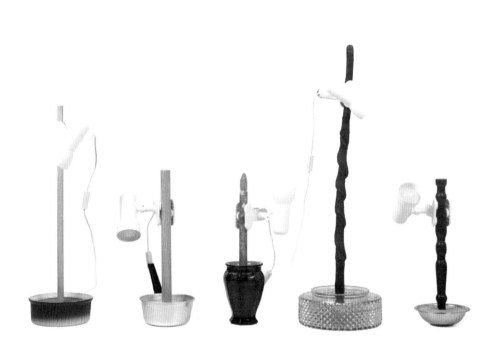

Cuisine d'Objets by 5.5 designers

Such an approach to design and production is inherently optimistic. It allows for a new definition of the role of the designer – someone who shifts their focus from the shaping of objects to the shaping of productive experiences. Cuisine d'Objets makes design a shared creative process. The completed object embodies the personality of its creator, as well as the insight of the designer. Ordinary objects are sublimated and redefined.

Turn to page 112 to read more about the philosophy behind Cuisine d'Objets, and how to make your own Cuisine d'Objets furniture.

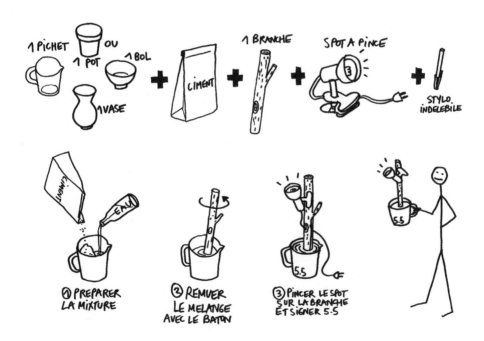

Cuisine d'Objets by 5.5 designers

\04: A simple clamp spotlight can be attached to any type of stem (be it wood, metal, or plastic) that has an appropriate thickness.

tide

by Stuart Haygarth
Photographs courtesy of Stuart Haygarth

For many years, designer Stuart Haygarth collected synthetic debris that washed up on a stretch of the coastline in Kent, England. He assembled a collection of transparent objects – mostly plastic – into a sphere form by hanging each piece of debris on monofilament fishing line with a split shot weight. The lines hang from a 1.5-metre-square board, and a 100-watt incandescent bulb shines from the centre of the sphere.

Many of the plastic items suspended in Tide are fragments. Recent analysis of the so-called 'great garbage patches' in the world's oceans has discovered that plastic debris is breaking up into small, widely dispersed fragments that are easily ingested by marine animals.

\01: The sphere is 1.5m in diameter and reaches a depth of 2.1m from the hanging board.

Components of the sphere include bottles, eyewear, beach play equipment, brushes and combs, lighters, lengths of hose, and a variety of plastic containers. The sphere is a reference to the moon, which affects the tides that in turn wash up the debris. Tide can be viewed as both a work of art and the document of a scientific survey – a study of the serious and mounting problem of plastic rubbish in the ocean.

The work of designer Stuart Haygarth (London, UK) aims to give banal and overlooked objects a new significance. Since 2004, Stuart has been working on design projects that revolve around the collection of objects. He typically gathers objects in large quantities, categorises them, and assembles them in a way that transforms their meaning. Chandeliers, installations, and functional and sculptural objects are the result. Portrait courtesy of Stuart Haygarth.

www.stuarthaygarth.com

\02: The transparent and translucent detritus is hung in a layered formation, as though the objects are suspended in water.

recycled tube light

by Castor

Photographs copyright Derek Shapton

Strict regulations exist for the disposal and recycling of used fluorescent tubes due to the presence of mercury within them. Canadian studio Castor designed a way to extend their lifespan while dramatically altering the quality of light that emanates from them. The Recycled Tube Light is literally a tube of tubes; burnt-out fluorescent tubes are clamped around steel rings, and lit from within by halogen bulbs.

\01: The light is produced in lengths of 2ft (0.6m), 4ft (1.2m), and 8ft (2.4m). It can be detailed for horizontal or vertical hanging, or freestanding use.

The bright light that shines consistently from the length of a regular working fluorescent tube gives way to dim and bright zones in the Recycled Tube Light. A tangle of red electrical cords plugs into the top of the light, drawing attention to the altered pattern of use. The tubes are obtained from significant Toronto buildings and institutions such as the Old City Hall, the University of Toronto, and the Toronto-Dominion Centre (which was designed by Mies van der Rohe).

Castor (Toronto, Canada) is Brian Richer and Kei Ng. The studio creates uncommon objects – often by recontextualising used materials – and also undertakes spatial and graphic design. Recently, Castor has worked on projects with interior designers and architects, creating custom light installations and furniture. Brian trained as an architectural stone carver and studied English literature and philosophy at York University. Kei studied architecture at the University of Winnipeg prior to many years art directing films and running a restaurant. Portrait by Jessica Eaton.

www.castordesign.ca

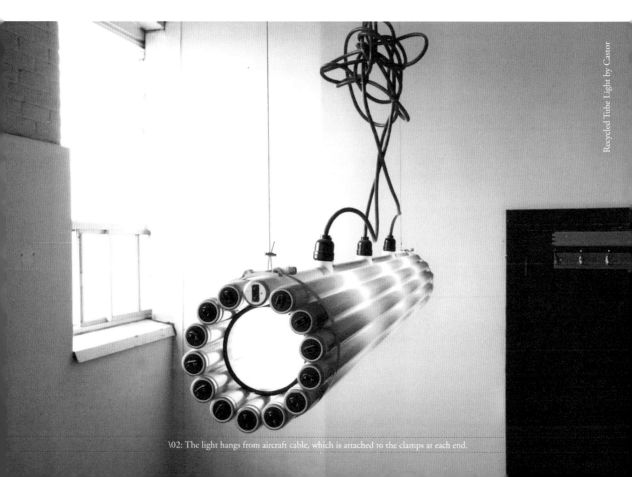

\02: The light hangs from aircraft cable, which is attached to the clamps at each end.

Recycled Tube Light by Castor

louis 900

by Reddish Studio

Photographs by Dan Lev and Reddish Studio

Louis 900 is a series of table lamps that gives familiar furniture forms a new function and character. The lamps are made with the legs of discarded chairs, stools, and tables of various periods and origins. The legs are turned upside-down and rest on 300-millimetre lengths of the apron (or board) that stretches between the legs of the original seat or table. Drum-shaped aluminium shades give the lamps a contemporary feel.

\01: Different paint colours bring variation to the series. Cut timber edges are left unpainted – a reminder of a past life.

The different antique styles (which include but are not limited to the French Louis XIV, XV, and XVI styles) bring their own stories to the design. The designers explained how they named the series as follows: "We heard a woman trying to describe her antique-style wedding dress. She said it was 'very extravagant, in the style of Louis 900.' We loved the new term, and adopted it for our lamp."

Designers Naama Steinbock and Idan Friedman founded Reddish Studio (Sitriya, Israel) in 2002. The studio produces a variety of objects including furniture, lighting, home accessories, and jewellery. No matter the type of object, Naama and Idan strive to infuse each one with its own character – something with which people can find a personal connection. Photograph by Shay Ben-Efraim.

www.reddishstudio.com

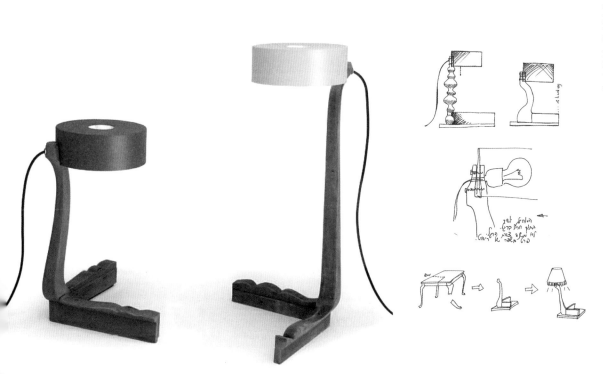

Louis 900 by Reddish Studio

\02: The furniture is found in flea markets and second-hand stores. A simple set of actions transforms each leg into a light.

trashlamps

by Godspeed
Photographs by Godspeed

Godspeed makes furniture, lights, and other products with an unorthodox, down-to-earth style. The objects are made with raw scrap materials. This draws attention to the idea of decay – as do the forms of the objects. "The beauty of scrap material is the imperfection, the lack of order," says Godspeed. "The undesirable becomes the desirable."

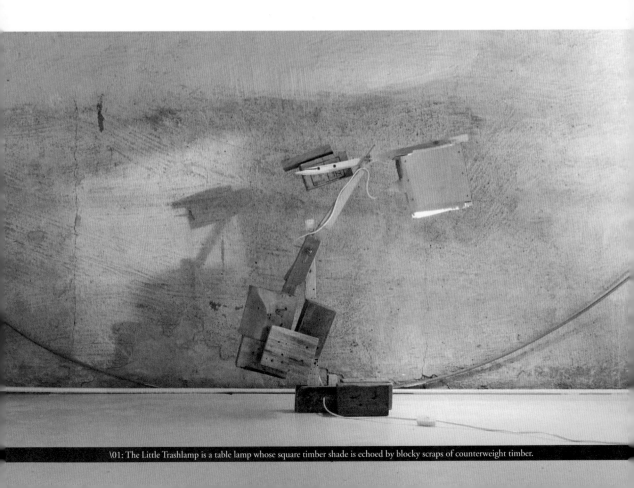

\01: The Little Trashlamp is a table lamp whose square timber shade is echoed by blocky scraps of counterweight timber.

The materials themselves guide the designers to their final design solutions. The Trashlamps (and other Trash furniture) are part of a working theory that the designers have called 'Wrong is the New Right' – an exploration of how much 'wrong' can be made 'right.' The Trashlamps are compositions of scrap timber, with accumulations of blocks and planks constituting counterweights on the ends of swinging arms.

Godspeed (Stockholm, Sweden and Tel Aviv, Israel) was established in 2008 when Joy van Erven (of the Netherlands) and Finn Ahlgren (of Sweden) met at a bar owned by Joy in Tel Aviv. They combined their knowledge of fine arts (Joy) and interior architecture and furniture design (Finn) to develop Godspeed as a statement on contemporary design. They take a conceptual approach to design, eliminating the sketching phase and producing every piece by themselves.

www.weareonlyinitforthemoney.com

Trashlamps by Godspeed

\02: The slender proportions of the Standing Trashlamp are reflected in the strips of timber that compose its counterweight elements.

index of objects

Classified by Upcycled Material

index of designers

Classified by Country

Acknowledgements

The compilation of *Upcycle!* has been an inspiring process of discovery, and we hope the same experience is had by the book's readers. an\b editions expresses its gratitude to the many designers and artists who have contributed their exciting work to the publication. We thank them for granting us insights into the fascinating stories behind the objects. We also express our gratitude to the photographers who have allowed us to feature their shots. *Upcycle!* is the third title produced by an\b editions.